RUNNER'S GUIDE TO CROSS COUNTRY SKIING

by Dick Mansfield

ACORN PUBLISHING

P.O. Box 7067 Syracuse, NY 13261-7067

Cover photo of skier courtesy of Salomon/Team Russell

Library of Congress Cataloging-in-Publication Data
Mansfield, Dick, 1940-
        Runner's Guide To Cross Country Skiing /
Dick Mansfield.
        2nd ed.

        Includes bibliographical references.
        Includes index.
    ISBN 0-937921-49-1
        1.Cross-country skiing.   I. Title
GV855.3.M36   1990   89-17754
796.93'2   CIP

Printed in the United States of America
10 9 8 7 6 5 4 3 2

Contents

 # 1. Getting started

Another dark November workout. Wind-driven sleet pelts your face as you run your daily route, and you think, "I've got four more months of this stuff to put up with."

If you live and run in the "snow belt," November through April is a series of challenges. Short days, icy roads, and encroaching snowbanks make running difficult and dangerous. Yet, most of us still head out the door every day. Neither rain, nor snow, nor sleet will keep us from our appointed rounds.

But as more and more runners are learning, there is a great alternative to slogging through the slush: cross country skiing. One of North America's fastest growing outdoor sports, cross country skiing provides the runner with an excellent complement to a year round running program. Not only does it give one of the better cardiovascular workouts of any exercise, skiing relieves the jarring of daily running while it helps build upper body strength. And it just might make you a better runner in the spring. St. Lawrence coach Paul Daly, who has won masters championships in cross country skiing and is an accomplished runner as well, says, "Cross country skiing is not just an alternative, it is a way to really improve your running."

A number of runners, many from Switzerland and Scandinavia, have excelled in skiing as well as running. Ingrid Kristiansen was on the Norwegian ski team and won three silver medals in national championships before deciding to concentrate on her running. Gabriele Andersen, who has won the Great American Ski Chase series, has long been a top runner and skier. Many runners have used cross country skiing in their off-season workouts, runners including including Jacqueline Gareau (who once completed the 100 mile Canadian Ski Marathon), Grete Waitz, Dick Beardsley, and Hal Higdon.

Some top runners XC ski

Grete Waitz, here shown with the author, is a long-time nordic skier

Markus Ryffel, the Swiss runner who won the silver medal with a 13:07 5,000 meters at the 1984 Olympics, used cross country skiing for years. In 1980, while training in Oregon, he was unable to run due to an injury but could ski without pain. As a ski coach said, "His technique was ragged but he just worked hard at it. We smoothed him out and although he had never raced much on skis, he went down to California and finished fifth that year in a big 25K." Ryffel used skiing in December and January as the main part of his training and began a transition back to running in February.

Many top collegiate runners have traditionally run cross country or track and skied in the winter. Dorcas DenHartog, competing for Middlebury College, won the Division III 1985 NCAA women's 5000 meters cross country race and in 1986, finished 4th (2nd American) in the NCAA cross country skiing championships. At the 1988 Calgary Winter Olympics, she had the best U.S. individual nordic finish.

Runners who cross country ski shrug off the lousy running days of late fall for they know that better days are just ahead. Their "other season" is about to begin. Cross country skiing turns winter from tolerable to downright enjoyable.

Icy roads and encroaching snowbanks can make winter running difficult and dangerous

Cairn Cross, who worked for the U.S. Ski Association (USSA), says, "When I see runners out slogging through six inches of new snow, I want to stop the car, roll down the window, and ask if they've tried cross country skiing."

That's what this book will do — roll down the window to

shout that there's a great winter world out there for northern runners who choose to ski. There's no need to hang up the "waffle-stompers" but there is a chance to give the legs and running shoes a few days off, by learning how to weave skiing workouts into a running schedule. Regardless of your present competence in skiing, whether you have just thought about cross country skiing, or have been out touring a few times, or even are becoming fairly proficient on the slats, in the following pages you will learn about skiing from a runner's viewpoint.

Why Ski?

The running boom of the 1970s and 1980s was launched by Frank Shorter's dramatic marathon victory at the 1972 Olympics, an event watched on television by people across the continent. A similar phenomenon took place only four years later at the 1976 Winter Olympics when a young Vermont skier, Bill Koch, surprised the world and won a silver medal, the first medal ever garnered by an American in Olympic cross country skiing competition. His success triggered an explosion in the cross country business. This growth spurt brought thousands of novice skiers into the sport. Like the running boom, the growth in nordic skiing has leveled out, yet each winter, cross country skiing gains more serious enthusiasts. Runners, cyclists, canoeists, and triathletes use the sport for a winter training alternative. As runners have cut back on the high mileage months and concentrated more on the quality of their running, some have looked for cross training opportunities. Cross country skiing presents an ideal substitute. By the same token, running prepares you well for nordic skiing — it is the basic training tool for most serious skiers.

Bill Koch started it

Avoid Overuse Injuries

Physicians and runners agree — cross country skiing is very gentle on the legs and joints. Dr. Edward Hixson, a sports medicine authority, says, "There are fewer over-use injuries associated with skiing. The incidence is much higher with running. A runner may strike the heel with three times his body weight, where with skiing he rarely exerts more than 1 1/2 times his body weight with nowhere near the impact. Most runners will find that if they do have over-use problems with the lower extremities, the problems will go away when they get on snow and get skiing." Dean Anderson, a Wyoming runner, put it like this: "Minor leg problems exacerbated by constant running disappear virtually overnight when I switch to skiing in the late fall."

Minor injuries disappear

This relief is especially appreciated by masters runners. Ed Buckley, nationally ranked (65-69) in running, is also a medal-winning nordic skier. He says, "Skiing's a great thing for the body — you get away from all that pounding for a while. It's a real nice change."

Cross country skiing is a good change-of-pace for runners who have worked all summer and fall on the roads, perhaps finishing with a marathon. It's a nice mental break from a regime of constant road work and gives one something to look forward to. Runners who cross country ski look forward to snow-covered roads because they know that instead of pavement pounding, they'll soon be gliding on skis.

Take a mental break

John Dimick, with a 2:15 Boston finish and a win in the New Orleans marathon to his credit, has used cross country skiing as a training supplement. Dimick, a Vermont runner who has retired from the elite racing scene, feels that many "snow belt" runners could benefit from skiing. "Why beat yourself?" he asks. "Why not take some of the drudgery out of training? Use the winter to your advantage."

He knows whereof he speaks. Back in the late 1970s when he was competing seriously, he spent about one-third of his winter training time on cross country skis. "I came out of that year with real good strength — it took me about a month to get back into full running shape. That was the spring I finished thirteenth at Boston."

For snowbound runners, skiing provides not only a chance to focus on a different aerobic endurance activity, it also presents a chance to be refreshed, both physically and mentally. Dick Kendall, a nationally-ranked runner in the 55-59 age group says, "For me, skiing is a change of pace. It's poetry for the soul."

Cross country skiing can be "poetry for the soul"

And for others, skiing generates enthusiasm because it has opened up a whole new world of PRs. "I've pretty well topped out in running," notes masters runner Doug Allen, a 45-49 runner with a sub-37 10K best. "I've been competing in cross country skiing for only a year but I'm setting PRs in every race. I love it."

Improve Overall Fitness

Cross country skiing is generally recognized as the most effective cardiovascular exercise. You can gain more aerobic conditioning from skiing because skiing involves a larger percentage of the body than running. It is able to place heavier demands on your aerobic capacity. World class cross country skiers have been compared with other international athletes and were found to have the highest maximal oxygen uptake (VO2 max) of the group. (To review briefly, maximum oxygen uptake is a measure of the output of the heart multiplied by the oxygen content of the blood. As a person gets in better shape, the number of oxygen-carrying red blood cells increases.) The elite skiers were found to be the best at providing and metabolizing oxygen.

But don't conjure up a picture of an exhausted ski racer hunched over his ski poles, panting and ready to vomit. In spite of skiing's excellent aerobic workout, it's far from being a treadmill test on snow. Bob Hinman, a 58-year old runner who took up skiing in his early 50's, completed his first ski marathon (31 miles) in a little over six hours. The next day he was up before dawn for a sunrise ski tour with his wife and in the afternoon took a five mile run. "I can't believe how great I felt," he reported.

The demands of cross country skiing come in spurts and while you can get a good anaerobic test climbing a steep hill, you can also get a welcome rest on the downhills. In fact, for a while, until you get your techniques polished, you may find it hard to get a good solid ski workout in the time you have available. That is one reason why most runners who ski still run a few days each week all winter. Not only do they keep their specific running muscles tuned up, they also get a quick efficient workout. Coaches suggest that you run short to medium distances at a moderate pace during your weekly runs. Many runner/skiers either alternate workouts or run during the week and ski during the weekend.

Plan to run all winter

So whether you want to rest injured running muscles, fight the doldrums of winter, or just maintain or improve your fitness during the cold weather months, the world of cross country skiing awaits. As a runner, you are in better shape than most beginning skiers before you even bend over to latch on a pair of skis. With some work — which turns out to be fun — you can use that good conditioning to get going and to get running on skis. Cross country ski season generally runs from January to March in most of the northern states but, in some areas, we can ski as early as November and as late as April. Obviously, a lot depends on the weather. It pays to be ready to go when the snow hits. Runners who decide to take up skiing have a few choices to make before they ever strap on skinny skis. Get these choices out of the way early so that you can get the most out of the ski season once it arrives.

Buy Or Rent?

The first decision a runner faces about skiing is this: "What do I do about equipment?" This subject will be discussed in greater detail in the next chapter but the choice basically comes down to a "buy or rent" decision. Here are some factors that a runner should consider when getting started:

1. How much money do I have to spend initially?
2. Where will I be doing my skiing?
3. How often will I be skiing?
4. How close is a reputable cross country center?
5. How easy am I to fit, size-wise?

Many articles on cross country skiing recommend that you rent equipment a few times to see whether you will like the sport enough to justify an investment in equipment. That is not a bad idea, but in general, renting doesn't work for most runners. Here's why. Most of us run every day and set up routines and stick with them. The same goes for skiing — we want to get out and get exercising. If getting ready to ski turns out to be too much of a hassle, we'll simply tie up the the running shoes, go out, and trudge through the slush. We're not going to drive somewhere to rent gear only to find that "all the size 9's are gone" or that there is a big crowd waiting to be fitted. So, one of the barriers to renting for runners is convenience. The other barrier to renting ski equipment concerns the quality and condition of the gear. For runners interested in performance skiing as an exercise supplement, rental equipment will not give you a true picture of what skiing is all about. Most rental equipment, while safe and adequate, is not what you will end up skiing on. The touring skis will most likely be waxless, the boots and bindings the older style 75mm, and the poles flimsy. It is fine equipment for beginners but is slow, heavy gear. It's a little like going out for a run in a pair of borrowed Nikes that a friend has used to train for a couple of marathons.

Plan to buy skis

Regardless of what books and articles and your friends say, do not be afraid to step right out and buy your own ski equipment. For a runner who wants to take advantage of the winter, it is a safe investment. You can find out how to buy the right ski gear in Chapter 2.

Where To Ski

Just as we are free to run on a limitless variety of roads and trails, so it is with cross country skiing. For many who ski, this "getting away from it all" is what nordic skiing is all about. Unlike those who choose downhill skiing, cross country skiers are not dependent upon ski areas or ski lifts — or the costs that come with them. We can ski wherever there is snow.

Runners who plan to use skiing as a training tool will want to find a place to ski with prepared trails. In order to get a good workout on high performance skis, having a good set of tracks and groomed trails is important. (If you plan to skate, tracks are of lesser importance but you still want packed snow.) Yet, you can, as I do, cut your own trail and ski it and ski it until it becomes packed. A friend goes one step further, and drags a 2x4 plank behind him across the school soccer field, grooming his own workout area as he goes along.

There are hundreds of ski touring centers that have sprung up since the 1970s. Some are major complexes with hundreds of kilometers of trails, others are associated with alpine ski areas, but the majority are small "mom & pop" type operations. There are many advantages to skiing at a center: the trails are groomed and tracks usually set, instruction is available, and there is often a place to come in out of the cold and warm up. It is also a good place to give the sport a try by renting before deciding to buy. Trail fees are very reasonable, often about $6 a day, and more and more areas feature night skiing as well as snowmaking. The drawbacks of paying to ski, aside from having to drive to the site, may be crowded trails. This is especially true on weekends. Runners trying to learn a new sport may be frustrated enough with their balance problems and not need to deal with tracks clogged with slow skiers. But, if you pick your spot and your time, you can find plenty of room to ski. Kevin Kearney is a masters runner who also is a competitive ski racer. "I ski every night on a lighted loop in my town," he says. "It's like having my own training site."

There are many other places to ski. State and national forests have miles of trails available to ski touring. Some hiking trails can be skied during the winter but be cautious

Find a
local
place to
ski

—just because a ranger tacked up a "Ski Trail" sign at the trailhead doesn't mean that the trail is within the ability of a novice. The best bets are those trails that follow old logging roads or fire lanes. Snowmobile trails are also excellent possibilities for cross country skiers. In some states, skiers join the snow machine clubs and help maintain the trails. Chapter 7 will discuss ski touring in more detail.

The trails at touring centers can get crowded on weekends

When To Ski

All it takes is about six inches of snow and you can be skiing. On the first few outings of the year, carry a plastic scraper along because the ground is often not yet frozen and your ski bottoms can easily collect mud and ice. Early in the season, it is easy to ruin the bases of your skis — most skiers have an old pair of "rock" skis that they use for early training runs. They haul them out again in the spring when rocks and dirt reappear.

For those of us who work during the day, the short days and early darkness present problems for skiing. Yet it is not unlike the problems we face as runners, and we tackle them the same way. Some runners, content to work on their skiing in daylight, run during the week and ski on the weekend. Others take an afternoon here and there to work on their cross country technique. Others frequent ski centers with lighted trails. Headlamps can work well for skiing and nights with a full moon are like skiing in daylight. Anyone who has figured ways to run outside all winter will have no problem devising ways to ski.

Carve out time to ski

It takes a while to become proficient on skis. Don't plan to use skiing as a complete replacement for conditioning — use your runs to get your "aerobic fix" and use your ski time to work on technique. Once you get comfortable on skis and if there's reliable snow cover, you can take a complete break from running and ski every day.

Cross country skiing can be a great leveler of abilities — it is a sport, like hiking, where one can go out with family and friends and still get in some training. Just make it a tour, not a tough workout. If you need a little extra activity, break trail for the group or charge up the hills a few more times. Runners will find that being able to ski with friends and family is a nice cross country bonus.

So while cross country skiing is not going to lower your 10K time by 20% or get you ready for the Boston marathon, it might just provide a new dimension in your athletic life. I ski because it is more mentally demanding than running and easier on legs that are half a century old. Skiing is a skill sport — you don't just put your head down and go — so there's a good chance, with practice and study, to make dramatic improvements. And it does help stay in shape for the spring. Dave Jones, a fine masters runner from upstate New York says, "All the little injuries I pick up during the summer and fall heal during ski season. I go into spring in better shape than most of the guys I run against, and I surprise a few of them every spring."

Skiing is a skill sport

2. Gearing up

Think about your first running outfit and how it compares with your gear today. For many runners, cutoffs, grey sweats, and sneakers comprised the "start-up" gear. Now, the basic equipment of most serious runners consists of nylon shorts and singlets, weather-proof warmups, and several pairs of good running shoes. Many of today's skier/runners started the same way — jeans and windbreakers over long underwear for clothes and a starter set or rentals for ski equipment. Later, they upgraded.

At some point, if you plan to get serious about skiing, you'll want to buy your own equipment. First of all, there is some good news for runners: much of your winter running gear — tights, windsuits, gloves, and hat — is perfect for skiing. But that is the easy part. If you thought selecting a pair of running shoes was difficult, wait until you walk into a ski shop and come face to face with an array of skis, poles, boots, and binding systems. Here is some help on how to proceed.

What To Buy

Buying ski equipment is a lot like choosing running shoes — you tend to get what you pay for. While most of us may have difficulty noticing a difference in performance between a pair of $45 shoes and a $90 pair, doubling the price with a pair of skis results in a marked degree of improvement. If you buy low-price discount store ski equipment, you very well may be disappointed by the performance. It's like trying to run in cheap sneakers — your body knows the difference.

Ski equipment can be divided into several categories. First on the rung is the economical starter package, priced at about $100, featured in virtually all ski shops and department stores. This gear, as you might expect, is low quality and often carryover equipment from years past. While it can get you started, it also can turn you off from skiing altogether. The skis in low-cost packages are usually "doggy" — their bases are slow or else the no-wax pattern is not effective. They tend to be "soft," lacking the camber needed to support an active runner/skier. The poles are flimsy and tend to lose tips and baskets, and the boots are heavy.

Cheap skis are slow skis

However, if you've got a "bare-bones" budget, you can get up and going with an inexpensive package — just remember that you may get frustrated with them. Look at it as a short-term purchase to be upgraded in a year or two. Then the discount skis can make a great second pair to be used when rocks and mud abound. Discount packages can also work for kids, who will outgrow cheap sets as fast as they will expensive ones. Still, think twice about low cost gear and take a hard look at the next level of equipment which is faster, more responsive, and more suited to an active athlete.

Just as runners ponder the choice of training shoes and racing flats, or a combination of the two, skiers face three categories of equipment — touring, light touring, or racing. (Many ski shops will also carry mountaineering skis and telemark equipment.) Touring skis are wide, stable, and can be used for track skiing as well as "across the hills and dales" exploring. The next general category, light touring, fits many runners. Available in the package price range of around $200 to $250, these skis will be more responsive and easier to handle. Many are "combi" skis which can be used for the two basic techniques, traditional and skating, as well as for entry-level citizen racing. Light touring equipment is available in complete packages or can be set up in a "mix and match" arrangement by most good ski shops and mail order operations.

Consider light touring gear

Are you the type of runner who dives into a new sport headfirst — do you covet a Kevlar canoe for triathlons, do you want to upgrade that bike? If the answer is yes, you should think about starting right out with racing skis, just to avoid having to upgrade later on. You'll need a packed surface for racing skis; they are not made for tromping through the wilds. Sure, the gear is a little "squirrelly" but once you get the hang of it, you'll love the fun of performance skiing. Some coaches feel that light racing gear is no more difficult to learn on than wider touring equipment. It is a lot like cycling — you can learn the finer points of riding just as easily on a $900 Cannondale as a $90 K-Mart special. And what a difference in responsiveness! When picking ski gear, keep in mind that if you like to road race now, you'll probably jump into some ski races. Don't be afraid to spend a little extra because it will pay off in the end.

Racing skis are light and responsive

Where To Buy

You'll hear about real bargains at ski swaps and lawn sales but until you know what to buy, I suggest that you look elsewhere. Likewise, until you are savvy about equipment selection, steer away from the stores that promote with price — their motive is to get their ski gear out the door — they may not be too fussy about getting the right equipment on the right person. Ski coach Roger Weston says, "Many ski shops don't keep up with what's going on. They sell skis too long and poles too short. You walk in the door and they say, 'Well, you look like a pair of 215's will fit you.'"

Buy at a good shop

Seek out a reputable shop, a "specialty shop," and talk to the folks — they should be willing to take the time with you. You may have to pay a little extra for that, but it is worth it to know that your skis have the right camber for you and that your bindings are on to stay. Do some homework on your own — talk to skiers, read the product reviews in *Cross Country Skier*. See if there is a nordic ski club in your area and talk to some of the members. (Many ski shops give club members discounts of 10-15%.)

Few shops that carry a lot of alpine (downhill) ski gear have good cross country departments. Look for places that sell bikes, canoes, or backpacking gear and that have salespersons who are skiers, preferably ski racers. Go see them during off-peak hours and talk to them about your plans — that you want to ski for alternate exercise, may want to race, and have limited funds. They should be able to select gear that fits you and your budget. The shop should mount the bindings for you and get everything ready to go.

Check out mail order selection

If you don't have good nordic shops in your area, you might give one of the mail order firms listed in the Resources section a try. Their equipment selection is more extensive than all but the largest ski shops and they ship orders out the same day. Some can give you technical selection advice over the phone and then set the equipment up for you. If you decide to order your gear by telephone, latch on to a knowledgeable skier before you dial so that you have an good idea of what to order.

When To Buy

Late summer or early fall is the time when you can often get the best price on ski equipment. Shops often have "carryover" goods that were either held over from last season or bought at the end of the season at a good discount to allow for early promotions. The other obvious time to shop for bargains is late spring, about the time ski shops are putting together bikes and looking for floor space. During the ski season, you can quite often buy ski packages of skis, bindings, boots, and poles, at a good savings off the items priced individually.

As in running, if you're shopping for the latest popular equipment, plan to pay list price or close to it. Some of this gear, being imported, is difficult to get in quantity so there will be little discounting. On the other hand, light touring gear, which might be a couple of years old in design, may be just what you need and be priced accordingly. So, while timing can affect price, the ski season is so short in much of the country that you might as well not wait but just go do it. Again, visit shops in off-hours and check for deals on complete packages. It doesn't hurt to ask.

What About Waxing?

Runners who decide to look at light touring or entry-level racing skis will have a basic decision to make — "Do I buy no-wax or waxable skis?" Ever since their introduction in the 1970s, waxless skis have appealed to many skiers because of their "strap 'em on and go" characteristics. For runners, it is as easy as lacing up a pair of running shoes.

Waxless skis, developed in the 1970s by Trak with the introduction of the now-famous "fishscale" pattern, have been pooh-poohed by skiing purists for years. The pattern the skis leave in the snow and the swishing sound they make during the glide has been considered the mark of a beginner. Yet, as in running, racers often show the way, product-wise, for the rest of us, and when Bill Koch gained **No-wax skis are popular** success with no-wax skis in Europe, suddenly these "beginner" skis gained respectability and began to sell. Even now, most elite racers carry a pair or two in their ski bag for special snow conditions. Presently, about three out of every four sets of skis sold in North America are waxless. The efficiency of the skis has improved as new designs are developed. Generally, they still are slower than waxed skis, but many runners will opt for convenience over a little extra glide.

Waxless skis come in many systems, each designed to provide the grip on the snow needed to push and glide. *Positive-based* skis have a pattern molded on the base of the ski so that the fishscale or diamond pattern (there are many variants) sticks out from the base to engage the snow. These skis work best on crusty and icy snow. *Negative-based* skis have a pattern cut into the base, somewhat like the tread on a snow tire, and are best for loose snow. There is also a wide array of chemical base and "hairy bases" which have mohair-like synthetic fibers under the foot. These systems, with proper pretreatment, are best suited for wet conditions. It helps to keep any no-wax ski clean and to wax the tips and tails with glide wax to improve overall performance.

Waxless skis can strike a happy medium for runners. They work well on uphills but are slower on the downhills and the flats. While they don't glide as well or climb as well as a pair of perfectly-waxed skis, they are much more efficient than a pair of skis with the wrong wax. And, as one runner friend of mine says, "The way I ski, I don't want to go any faster." One note of caution: if you are interested in learning to skate on skis, no-wax skis, because of their effective grip, will not glide well. But for runners who just want to get out and go, and probably won't race, waxless skis may well be the ticket. You don't tinker with your shoes for 15 minutes, why should you with your skis?

With waxed skis, wax provides the grip on the snow needed to do the diagonal stride, the primary technique used by most skiers. When your weight is on a waxed ski, snow crystals penetrate the wax and allow you to push off with that ski — the ski literally grips the snow. As the ski moves forward, the wax releases its hold and allows the ski to glide. This "grip and slide" is the key to proper waxing.

So, to wax or not to wax, that is the question. The feeling of a correctly waxed pair of skis can't be matched. They when climbing or pushing off. Improperly waxed skis are a pain and give you plenty of exercise — either you slip and slide or else you end up walking with half of the forest floor sticking to your skis. You can waste precious time fooling around with wax, time that could be spent on the snow getting in better shape. Yet waxing is part of the mental challenge of cross country skiing to many performance-oriented skiers.

Consider waxing for performance

Grip wax allows you to push off when doing the diagonal stride

Don't let skiers hype you about how difficult waxing is. Granted, there is a certain mystique, a certain lore, that is closely tied into the psyching done on the racing circuit; however, waxing is not difficult in most snow conditions. Wax manufacturers have made waxing easier with many new wide temperature range grip waxes which are easy to use. Wax systems are color coded and are covered in more detail in Chapter 10. One of the best sources on how to wax skis is John Caldwell's *The New Cross Country Ski Book*, which, packed with information, is now in its eighth edition. It should be part of your ski library. My original copy from 1971 is dog-eared and covered with klister wax from years of being toted around in wax kits.

The growing popularity of skating on skis (Chapter 5) for

You can't
skate on
no-wax
skis

performance skiing is moving serious skiers further away from no-wax skis. There is no need for a "grip zone" and, in fact, no-wax patterns drastically cut down the glide, making it hard to skate. If you plan to compete in citizen racing, you'll probably try skating. That alone may help you make a decision to not buy no-wax skis.

Basic Ski Terms — Leaning The Language

How do we find out what kind of running shoe to buy? Aside from reading some of the articles and the ads, have you ever gone up to a runner after a race and asked how he or she likes their running shoes? I do it quite often, especially when I spot someone of my build wearing what looks like a new model. Who wants to wade through terms like curved or straight last, heel counters, poly-you-name-it shock absorbing sole? Most of us just want to cut through the "techno-speak" and find a shoe that works.

It's the same way with skis. Do we really care whether our skis are made with injection molding or torsion box construction? What we need to know is what's the best ski for our athletic ability and pocketbook. It doesn't hurt to ask a few questions. When I'm looking for skis, I ask citizen racers how they like the racing skis they've got on, whether the skis are hard to handle, where they bought them, etc. Just like runners, skiers love to share that kind of information with newcomers to the sport.

You should expect ski store personnel to be able to talk about sidecut, camber, and flex. If they look bewildered when you mention these terms, you'd better look elsewhere. But, in order to ask intelligent questions and make an informed choice, runners should have a understanding of some of the ski lingo. If you want to dig into technical specifications of skis in more detail, several books in the Resource section will give more help. Here are the basics.

The *width* of the ski is measured in millimeters. Touring skis are wide, usually 50 to 55 mm since they need to support your weight in untracked snow. Light touring skis, more suited for packed areas, are narrower, about 48-50 mm. Racing skis are the narrowest, often only 44 mm wide.

The difference in the width of skis from tip to tail is called *sidecut.* You can easily see this by putting a pair of touring skis side by side on the floor — most likely the tips and tails will be touching but there will be a gap in the middle. That gap is the sidecut, and it ranges from zero for many racing skis to 10 mm for touring skis. Sidecut makes the ski turn easier because the tip and tails dig in when the ski is up on its edge.

For years, *length* of skis has been measured by the "arm-in the air" method. Many ski stores and rental shops still have you raise your arm and recommend that the tip of the ski come to your upraised wrist. Be careful. This method is pretty old-fashioned for today's skier, especially with skating becoming so popular. There is no handy formula that works — ski length depends upon not only your height but your weight and your athletic ability. (A heavier skier may use a slightly longer ski than a lightweight; a better skier will often use slightly longer skis.) Most men use skis that are 205 to 215 centimeters long, while those who skate use shorter skis (190 to 200 cm.) Many women ski on 180 to 195 cm skis. Don't buy skis that are too long because shorter skis are easier to handle and, according to some designers, faster.

Keep skis short

Camber is the arch of the ski that holds the patterned bottom or "grip wax" off the snow when you glide. *Flexibility* is what allows the ski to bend to grip the snow when you put your weight on it and push off. Flexible skis are called soft-cambered skis while stiffer skis are called, just that, stiff skis. In order to get proper performance out of your skis, the camber must match your weight and leg strength. If you have too soft a ski, you'll drag the middle section during the diagonal stride and cut into your glide — if your skis are too stiff, you'll slip and slide all day.

There are several ways to select the proper camber. The easiest is to squeeze the skis together. If you can do this with one hand, you've got a pair of soft cambered skis. Now try to squeeze a pair of racing skis together — you will probably find it impossible to completely close the gap between them. These skis have what is called "double camber," one camber but with a stiffer section in the middle. Most runners will find that they opt for light touring skis, which can usually be squeezed together with

27

both hands. The squeeze comparison is just that, a comparison between skis, not an absolute test.

Although some ski shops class it in the same category as the "raise-an-arm" system for ski length, the paper test still can be used to help select skis for camber. (It is, as will be mentioned later, also a way to determine the *wax pocket* for a pair of skis.) First, find an uncarpeted level floor, lay the skis on the floor and place a piece of paper under the skis at the point where the bindings go (the balance point). Then stand on the skis and have the salesperson or a friend move the paper. They should be able to slide it fore and aft about a foot to 18 inches. If you've pinned the paper to the floor, the skis are too limber which means you'll end up dragging the ski and getting more training than you bargained for. Conversely, if the ski is too far off the floor,

Use the paper test

your kick zone will never make enough contact with the snow and you will slip. When you place all your weight on one ski, as you would when "kicking" during the diagonal stride, the paper should be pinned to the floor.

Calibrated camber testers are used by some ski shops to match skis to skiers. These gauges measure the force it takes to close a pair of skis, sort of a mechanical squeeze test. The reading is then, using a chart for weight, matched up with a skier. These systems are used mostly for racing skis although most racers agree that because of each person's weight and leg power differences, the best way to select skis is to go out and ski on them. Good ski shops will help you with the decision. They may even have a pair of "loaners" of different widths and cambers that you can try out before making the final selection.

Skating skis have a stiffer forward section than traditional skis, allowing a constant pressure to be applied along the whole ski as you push off. Camber becomes of less concern if you plan to skate since you will be using the ski, not the grip wax, for propulsion. Sidewalls of skating skis are strengthened and the skis are shorter. But rather

Look hard at combi skis

than buy two pairs of skis, many athletes opt for a pair of combi skis, dual-purpose skis that can be used for both skating and traditional skiing. These might be just the ticket for an active runner. Most recreational skiers and citizen racers could care less if their skis have side cut or whether they have soft tips or stiff torsional flex. We want skis that will be comfortable, long-lasting, and will help us go for some age group awards. In spite of the "techno-speak," it is just like buying running shoes.

Boots And Bindings

Nordic boots have come a long way from the heavy leather touring boots that came in any color you wanted, as long as it was black. Now, purple and yellow high-topped skating boots adorn the feet of elite racers and a mind-boggling array of binding systems compete for your skiing dollars. Cross country boots, like running shoes, now catch the eye while providing better support then ever before. Boots parallel the ski categories: there are touring, light touring, and racing models. (You also can buy boots suited for mountaineering or telemark skiing.) Runners will generally lean toward the light touring or racing models, whether or not they plan to race. These boots are lighter and much more like running shoes in design and feel. Because they use new insulating materials, they also are a lot warmer to wear than the earlier models.

The new boot/binding systems are light and comfortable

29

Touring boots are still usually made of leather and still have the widest sole of the group and often a 75 mm toe. This classic boot design, along with the 3-pin "rat trap" bindings that fit it, have been on the scene for years and are still very common. If you rent skis, this is the system you'll often be handed. These inexpensive boots and bindings have served millions of skiers well for years and are still practical for the more rugged touring treks. They are a little heavy for track skiing although many good skiers, including some citizen racers, find that these old favorites fit the bill.

There is a bevy of boot/binding systems available for the runner/skier, ranging from light touring systems to stiff high cut skating boots. These are integrated systems which match the boot and the binding and provide excellent ski control. There are a half dozen common systems, which, in spite of the claims, are quite similar in design and feel. It's a little like tread design in running shoes. We buy the ones that are the most comfortable and feel "fast." It is the same with boots. Ski boots are sized using the European system so you will have to do some experimenting to get a correct size. Try them on with the same thickness socks you'll use while skiing. (I find that a wool athletic sock over a light poly sock works well for all but sub-zero conditions.) The boots should fit snugly with some room in the toe — if they're too tight your circulation can be cut off, resulting in cold feet; if the boots are loose, you will run the risk of developing blisters. If you have trouble with width or length, try another brand. Once you find one that feels good, get the binding that matches it.

Pick a boot system for the family

Look hard at one of the dual purpose boot/binding systems available. These are stiff enough for skating yet allow enough flex to diagonal stride. Also consider what your friends are wearing. It is fun to switch skis from time to time to check waxes and ski handling qualities. You need compatible bindings to do that. Likewise, keep the systems standard in the household. More than once, one of my sons raced on a pair of skis and then let Dad take them for the later masters race. Pick a system that is comfortable because ski boots, unlike running shoes, don't wear out very fast — you can ski with them for years.

Poles

Over a quarter of the thrust developed by an accomplished cross country skier comes from the ski poles. Runners realize this at once when, after skiing, they feel the tenderness in the triceps and other upper body muscles. Until recently, most of the ski poles that came with ski packages were bamboo (tonkin cane). These have been replaced by low-cost fiberglass poles which are stronger and more durable but still too flexible for performance skiers. Poles that flex are inefficient — some of your energy is lost in the bending. It pays to have a pair of poles that will be a help, not an energy drainer.

Runners who purchase light touring gear or who become interested in getting fast on skis will want to consider stiffer, stronger poles. These are usually made of stiff aluminum and sell for $50 to $75 a pair. Serious racers get into more exotic materials like Kevlar and carbon fiber for the shafts of their poles with prices well over $200.

You will see a lot of different baskets on poles. The traditional circular baskets are good for skiing in unpacked snow or for general touring. Skiers who frequent areas with groomed trails will want to look at the light half-basket poles. These are more efficient because the tip stays in the snow better during the end of the pole thrust. Racers use a variety of streamlined baskets, all of which are unsuited for general touring. While you are looking at baskets, notice the tips of the poles. They will be curved backwards which helps with the withdrawal of the pole from the snow.

For any but the cheapest ski poles, there will be a right pole and a left one. The straps give the clue. The top strap should be on the outside of your hand. (Mark your poles so that you don't have to figure out which is which when the wind is howling and you want to get exercising.) Poles should have a knob at the end and the straps should be adjustable.

Learn how to put on the pole straps in the warmth of the ski shop. Bring your hand up through the loop of the strap and grab the handle — you should feel the strap snug against your hand. As we will note in Chapter 4, the straps help develop power during poling and, properly adjusted, allow you to rest your hands during the backswing. (That's what the knob is for, it should rest easily between your thumb and forefinger as the poles are extended backwards at the end of the poling stroke.)

What length should your poles be? The standard method to determine pole length has been to have them come up to your armpits as you stand on a hard surface. For runners planning to compete, a slightly longer pair will help develop more power. Runners who plan to skate should use poles at least chin high, and probably close to nose high. (see Chapter 5.)

Splurge on good poles

Ski poles should be the best that you can afford — this is not the place to cut costs. Plan to end up with light stiff poles of adequate height, probably about shoulder height if you plan to try both traditional and skating.

Clothing

If you are a winter runner, you already own about everything you need to get out cross-country skiing. You are also aware of some of the dangers of winter running/skiing, the effect of wind chill, and the need to especially protect the extremities. If you are male, you also know the need for crotch protection in the winter. Wind chill becomes even more of a factor because of the speed you attain on downhill runs.

Skiing in a wind-proof warmup suit over underwear and a turtleneck does the trick in most skiing weather. It's a loose outfit, one that you probably already run in, and if you get too warm, you can tie the jacket around your waist. Likewise, your lycra running tights worn over long underwear will usually be right for many ski conditions. Use what you have — if it works for running, it will be fine for skiing. Just as in running, protect the extremities. A warm knit ski hat will help retain body heat, and you will find many racers wearing thin earmuffs as well.

Dress in layers

Dress in layers and dress for what you will be doing. If you are out for a tour with friends, dress as you would for a winter walk. On the other hand, if you are going racing, you can, just as in road racing, get by with a lighter outfit because of the body heat generated. Use the lessons you've learned from running — it is easier to shed extra clothes.

I carry a garbage bag folded up in my fanny pack to use for an emergency windbreaker and a pair of socks which can also double as extra mittens.

You will find that due to the poling action, your hands will most likely stay warmer than they do in running. Consider buying some cross country ski gloves which will help your poling. Shy away from the super thin racing gloves — it is easier to deal with sweaty hands than cold ones. Err on the side of warmth.

Knickers, knee socks, and a light parka used to be "in vogue" as the perfect cross-country outfit. While these are still fine for touring, many track skiers and most racers are choosing the new form-fitting one piece outfits. While a little flashy for some tastes, the outfits are not only functional, they are also comfortable. And for the runner who isn't quite ready for prime-time hot pink lycra, more conservative one-piece outfits are available. Nordic ski suits are great for workouts and citizen racing, but if you are on a tour, wear warmups or extra layers. The suits cool down fast as soon as you stop exercising.

The main trick to "gearing up" to ski is to first decide on a pair of skis of the right size and camber, pick a pair of poles of the right length and stiffness, and the rest is old news. We fit ski boots just as we do running shoes and can use use most of our running gear as is.

Skiing gives runners many things to add to the Christmas or Hanukkah wish list (Ms. Santa brought me a one piece racing suit not long ago.) You will want a fanny pack for lugging extra clothes and snacks, and a headlamp will allow you to go out skiing in the evening. Let's see, a waxing iron, a pair of polypropylene gloves, a pair of gaiters (to keep the deep snow out of your boots), and oh yes, Santa, a pair of ski stockings.

Skiing gift ideas

Runners can outfit themselves with used gear from a "ski-swap" for under $100 or can spend five to ten times that amount getting ready to go. In any case, get to know your specialty shop folks; they can be invaluable in steering you toward ski gear that will get you off and running — on skis.

3. Training for cross country skiing

Swedish ski coach Kjell Kratz is one of the most success-ful nordic coaches in the world. His skiers swept the Worldloppet marathon series from 1983 to 1985. In a ski clinic in the United States, he noted that many American coaches and skiers feel that bicycling is better for training for cross country skiing than running. Kratz doesn't agree. He believes that a solid running program, using hills and trails, is a better training method.

Cross country skiing has a lot in common with running and therefore doesn't require a lot of special training. In fact, a runner who has been running all season can start out on cross country skis right after the first snowfall and ski comfortably. Many do. These first few ski outings might bring out some tenderness in unused muscles, especially in the upper body, so other runners who plan to ski will go a step further and integrate some minor changes into their fall running program before they hit the ski trails. Others, with just a little extra effort, will train more specifically for cross country skiing.

As runners, we know it is easy to get obsessed with piling

up mileage. It can be comforting to be able to say, "Yes, I averaged 65 miles per week for the ten weeks before the marathon." But, just as runners have learned to get away from accumulating "junk miles" in their training, skiers likewise aim for quality in training. For most, there is only a limited amount of time available for workouts. Inclement weather and early darkness make it tough to find time to squeeze skiing workouts into the work week. "Canned" training formulas don't fit most people. Most of us need to find out what works for our situation — to aim for a combination of running and ski-specific workouts to use before the season and then, after snow arrives, a system of on-snow and off-snow training that will work throughout the winter.

Training With The Brain

In military flight training, student pilots are continually judged on an item called "headwork." Headwork is how one uses common sense before, during, and after a flight. It is a term well-suited for physical training as well — how we use our head may well determine how effectively we train, how well we use the limited time available to us, and how much fun we have while training.

Many articles have been written about the problems of overtraining, and many of us have been participants in the "mileage mania" that characterized the jogging boom. One writer put it like this: "At times it appears to me that the medal winners in our major competitions are not necessarily the most talented runners, but rather those with adequate talent who have survived their training programs." When we take up a new sport, be it biking, triathlons, or cross country skiing, it is easy to fall prey to overtraining when, with our enthusiasm for the new activity, we neglect to back off from our running. Instead of being complementary, the new sport places added stress on joints and muscles.

John Underwood is a former steeplechaser who, after studying exercise physiology in Finland, traded his running shoes in for ski boots and is now a highly successful ski coach. Having seen the way that the Scandinavians train for cross country skiing, he is convinced that North

Americans tend to work too hard at training. "We train too hard, too close to the anaerobic threshhold," he says, noting that anaerobic activity generates lactic acid at a rate faster than the body can handle it. "We don't do enough easy training. The Finnish skiers train from April to November, building an aerobic base. Only when they get on snow do they work on developing specific muscles." Underwood describes aerobic training as the building up of an aerobic reservoir which is then drawn upon as skiers race throughout the season. It is not unlike the training program that many running coaches espouse for running quality races — build the aerobic base and only then add some hill work, intervals, or Fartlek. If we have not raced too often or trained too hard, runners arrive at the start of the skiing season with a good aerobic reservoir.

Aerobic training goes by many names: base training, endurance training, or distance training. Regardless of what it is called, exercise physiologists and coaches suggest that runners and skiers do most of their training in the aerobic zone. In order to stay in the aerobic zone, you first need to estimate your maximum heart rate. One way for men is to subtract your age from 220 (226 for women), so for a 50 year-old man, the approximate maximum heart rate would be 170. The aerobic zone is about 60% to 80% of this or 102 to 136. Many coaches aim at 70% as a good training level (119). Exercising below this range range has, in the eyes of many experts, little training value. Exceeding it, which is easy to do in sprints, on hills, or during races, can actually detract from the aerobic base.

Estimate your aerobic zone

It is difficult, even for well-coached athletes, to train aerobically, to back off and stay in the aerobic zone while training. Prompted by the Seiko on the wrist, it is tempting to push it just a bit harder, to beat the last training run time by a few seconds. In skiing, since we are using the total body, it is even easier to overdo it. As one ski coach put it, "We need kinesthetic cues to reading our various limits, the kind of thing that runners have traditionally done by trial and error." One way to do it is to learn what breathing patterns correspond to a particular heart rate. Anaerobic threshold, for example is about the point where you are breathing hard but not gasping for breath.

37

Another monitoring method is to take your pulse during and after a workout. As you probably know from running, it is not always easy to do. It is even more difficult with ski poles and gloves to contend with. A better way is to use a heart rate monitor. More and more athletes, even "weekend warriors" who work out for fun and to keep their weight down, now use heart rate monitors. Now in a price range that is affordable by more runners and skiers, the devices are easy to use.

The first time I skied with a heart rate monitor, I learned that because skiing uses both upper and lower body muscles, it is easy to get the heart rate elevated. It is also therefore, easy to overtrain. It was something I had not thought too much about before that. The beeper on my wrist was set for 150 and sure enough, on every hill the thing began to beep. As I began to relax and think about how to keep in the training zone, I did better. A quick pause here, a little shift in ski cadence there, and I found that I was using my head, training with the brain.

Try a heart rate monitor

Keep your heart rate within the aerobic zone while training

What sort of a training program do I use? A friend of mine, planning to open a fitness center, promised that if I would join his club, that he would guarantee to take minutes off my 10K time. Then with a smile, he said, "Of course, first thing you've got to do is quit your job."

So it is with so many of the training programs written up for runners or skiers. Designed by the elite runner/skier, they assume that we have plenty of time, perfect weather, and a fat checkbook. "Cookbook" training programs simply do not work for most runner/skiers — we've got too much else cooking in our lives.

So the trick is to train aerobically, to tailor a personal workout program, and to weave some ski-related activities into our roadwork. This chapter will cover some training equipment and routines that can get you ready for cross country skiing. Fortunately, the easiest way to train for skiing is to do just what you've been doing — running.

Set up your own training plan

Train To Ski By Running

As every runner knows, one of the best features of running is that it is an efficient use of time. You can get aerobic fast and get a good workout in — that's why it forms a major part of most elite skiers' dryland training programs. The quadriceps, "quads" as the bikers say, are the muscles in the front of the upper part of the leg and are important to cross country skiing. You can work on these muscles by running hilly terrain. Serious skiers, like serious runners, run hills. Many coaches recommend that their skiers use leaping, bounding strides up the hill to imitate the diagonal stride movement. For ski-skating, skiers bound more off the inner leg muscles and don't run directly up the hill but rather run from side to side as they climb.

Run on ski trails

For most runner/skiers, just running a rolling course on soft ground will be more suitable than intervals and repeats. Another good way to condition your legs for skiing is to run cross country in the fall. Run some of the same trails you will ski later to get a sense of the terrain. If you like to compete, find a couple of cross country meets in your area — they will give you plenty of hills.

One caution: be aware of hunting seasons. They start

very early in many parts of the country. Runners in upstate New York and Vermont, my training locales, have to contend with bird hunters and bow-wielding deer hunters in early October. Think about adding a new aerobic routine **Be wary of** to your fall runs — talk or yell, or even sing, as you run in **hunters** the woods. I'd rather be considered a little whacko by a hunter than be mistaken for game. Wear your fluorescent vest and red clothing. Do not wear white, it can easily be mistaken for a deer's tail moving through the woods. Once regular season opens for deer, avoid running in the woods altogether.

Running With Ski Poles

Cross country skiing uses the upper body as well as the legs — that is one reason it is such an efficient workout. In order to get ready to ski, it is a good idea to incorporate some strength techniques into your running program in the fall. One way to do this is to run with weights, using a system like Heavy-Hands®. A much better way is to run with a pair of ski poles — it not only helps build strength, it gets you used to the rhythm of skiing.

Hank Lange, a fine triathlete and masters ski racer says, "Runners can get off the roads and run with poles in the woods. The varying terrain is a nice break. I run with my poles up hills or sometimes I just hike. It not only gives you a whole new perspective on your running, it also benefits both your running and your skiing."

Find an old set of poles of the right height (try just a little shorter than armpit high.) You can pick up used poles for **Find some** running at rental shops or ski/skate exchanges. Many **old poles** families have attics full of old poles that came with "starter sets" so check with your skier friends. Cut off the ski pole baskets to avoid entanglements in the woods, and you are ready to go.

Unless you live in the middle of ski country where folks are used to seeing skiers readying for the season, you may feel a bit self-conscious clacking down the road with a pair of poles. It brings out the wit in every local half-wit. Start off on trails and woods if you can, so that you can have a private spot to get started. The softer terrain is easier on your arms and legs as well.

The easiest way to train with poles is to run naturally and just gently plant the pole when it is ready, about every other stride. I find that my ski pole comes down about every two strides — in other words, my right pole strikes once for every two strikes of my right foot. If it doesn't work out quite like that, it's no big deal; the idea is to let your arms swing normally, just like you do when you ski. You will find that it is more tiring than straight running, even though the ski poles are light. Run your normal routes at your normal pace, or at first, even a little slower. Try not to concentrate on the poles, just let them come down naturally. After a few tries, your self-consciousness will vanish.

Run naturally

Try running some of the trails you'll ski later on

Many skiers concentrate on the hills when running with poles; some practice bounding up the hill, simulating the push off of the diagonal stride. Stride instead of run, or alternate between running and striding. It's easy to work on the double pole by planting the poles every third stride.

41

When running with poles, try to lift yourself up the hill with each pole plant, using your upper body to help propel you up the hill. The feeling will be very much like the thrust you'll get from your poles while skiing.

Aside from getting your upper body in shape, you'll get some side benefits — nasty dogs that harass you all year now find other things to do when you run by carrying ski poles. Poles also help your balance and traction when the leaves underfoot are wet or when the first slushy snows come. By the time skiable snow arrives, your ski poles will feel like old friends, and your arms and shoulders will be ready to tackle the hills in earnest.

Biking for Runners/Skiers

If you have brought bicycling into your training regime, you've gotten a good start to cross country training. Some elite skiers, having suffered more injuries from running in the off-season than they do from skiing, have made biking their preferred spring/summer aerobic workout. Nowadays, biking is increasing even more in popularity with nordic skiers because, being an exercise that builds the quads, it is quite specific training for ski-skating. The pace of biking — the work on the uphills and the recovery on the downhills — is also similar to skiing. Most coaches recommend that biking be used to get in the long distances needed to build a good aerobic base, rather than hammering the legs on long runs.

Cycling and skiing are alike

Mountain bikes, the 18-gear go-anywhere bikes that have become so popular, can fit right into the training program of many skiers. Much more durable than racing bikes, they can be used virtually anywhere and anytime. The hard climbs and thrilling descents give the summer rider a taste of cross-country skiing.

Try a mountain bike

Runners can also get a good workout on a wind trainer or stationary bicycle. You can read a book, watch television, or listen to heavy metal on a headset. But, for many, the boredom of inside biking is intolerable. But, biking, especially in the running season, is a viable option for many runners. It will help relieve their legs and joints during the running season and at the same time, ready them for cross-country skiing.

Mountain biking is a nice change of pace for runner/skiers

Roller Skis/Training Skates

Ever crested a hill in your car and encountered a skier skating toward you on roller skis? You see it more and more in ski country. Buying and using roller skis or training skates is a serious commitment toward skiing. If you shell out $200 for a pair, you may have made the transition from a runner who skis to a skier who runs. It happens every year to many runners — watch out!

Roller skis cost about $200-230

Roller skis have been used by serious skiers for years. They are a very specific training method, the closest thing to actual skiing, so they help with balance as well as

43

conditioning. Unless you get serious about ski racing, you'll be better off to run with poles or to bike. If you get interested in roller skis, get ones that have a ratchet arrangement that allows you to push off for the diagonal stride. You can use them for diagonal stride on uphills and for double poling on flats.

If you buy roller skis, get a pair that can be used for skating and diagonal stride

The Rollerblade® training skates, used by speed skaters and hockey players as well, are the choice of many competitive skiers for practicing ski skating and double poling. They are about $150 a pair.

You can use your regular ski poles for roller skiing but

Training skates are a favorite training method of the Canadian Ski Team

should replace the basket and the tip with a unit designed for the roads. Roller ferrules cost about $10 and have a carbide tip better suited for asphalt.

Speaking of which, it's no fun to meet asphalt "up close and personal." If you can, stay off the roads altogether. Use a school, factory, or church parking lot. Go there during off-hours to practice. Once you are comfortable, find some some hills to practice on. Do not roller ski downhill — there's no training gained and the risks of injury are obvious. It is safer and more beneficial to take off the skis and jog down, then ski back up.

If you get into roller skiing, work with a coach or a knowledgeable skier. You can pick up some bad habits in both diagonal stride and in skating using rollers, although these are easy to correct once snow comes. Get yourself video-taped and then work on technique while you train.

Roller ski races are a good summer workouts and one more type of competition for those so inclined. Some races use a mass start, while others use an interval start like a bike time trial. Roller skis vary greatly in speed— some roll more easily than others. It gives those of us who are back in the back of the pack a new excuse — "Darn rollers were slow."

Practice roller ski safety

Strength Training

Good cross country skiers often carry more weight than runners, in fact, some good ones look more like wrestlers than marathoners. That solid, powerful look comes from a strong upper body, something most runners lack. Much of the power in skiing comes from poling. Runners may want to do some specific training to get the upper body ready. The best exercises are those that simulate the movements of skiing. That is why running hills with ski poles is so beneficial.

Arm Strengtheners — Back before high-tech exercise devices were touted in glossy mail-order catalogs and inflight magazines, nordic skiers nailed old bicycle tubes to trees or posts and, standing as they would on skis, trained by yanking away. (Coach John Caldwell and his crew of national ski team members from southern Vermont pioneered the use of the inexpensive training aids in the late 1960s. In the lore of cross-country skiing, these tubes are known as "Putney arm bands.") While bike tubes or elastic bands certainly still work to simulate poling motion, there are several devices on the market that are lightweight and portable. Exer-Genie® is one of the more popular models (about $40).

Build upper body strength

Rollerboards — Another homemade training device, first used by the East Germans, is the rollerboard. It has been part of many a serious skier's workout routine since the mid-1970s. It consists of an inclined plywood ramp, a dolly with castered wheels, and a pair of ropes. You lie or kneel on the dolly and pull yourself up the incline with the ropes. A good description of how to make a roller board is in Bob Woodward's book, *Cross-Country Ski Conditioning*. With a couple of sheets of plywood, some 2 X 4's, and some wheels, rope, and fasteners, you're in business.

Weight Training — You don't need weights to do weight training — the roller board is a good example. Coach Hank Lange thinks that you should move your body instead of moving weights or pulleys. He suggests that you perform repetitions quickly, simulating the action you are going to perform. Pullups, situps, pushups, and roller board comprise the weight routine of many a good skier.

Less weight, more reps

Nautilus and Universal machines are excellent for conditioning runners for skiing. Nearly all stations are helpful; in fact, most coaches suggest that you use them all and not get too specific. Runners will find that the Super

Pullover machine is especially helpful for poling and the abductor/adductor machines are good for the skating muscles. Free weights, especially with low weights and high repetitions, are useful in building upper body strength. Get some coaching unless you are already competent in lifting.

Strength training should be done on easy days. If you run every day, take a run first and take it at an easy pace. Walk in and take a break before hitting the weights. Strength training should be done two or three times a week at the most.

Lift on easy days

Nordic Simulators — Pick up nearly any magazine and chances are you will see an ad for a nordic simulator. The two that are cited as being most specific to cross-country skiing are Nordic Track® and Fitness Master®. Both of these offer "jar-less" aerobic exercise and are generally considered to be effective for conditioning. The devices have their detractors and their supporters. Because either is a significant investment, it pays to check them out closely beforehand. Some fitness clubs have these machines along with Nautilus and Universal equipment. If you have barbells or an exercise bike gathering dust in the cellar, think twice before investing in a nordic simulator.

Training During Ski Season

Runners can train for skiing during ski season by continuing to run during the week and training on skis whenever time and weather permit. For most runners, this means most skiing is done on weekends, so it helps to have a couple of easily accessible places to ski. I have a couple of courses that I ski and, just like running season, I keep track of my time for each workout. Yet, times will vary: some snow is simply faster than other snow. It is best to measure your pace by how you feel — and train toward the side of taking it a little easier. As runners, we are not used to the overall effort of using arms and legs, and it is easy to get carried away a bit if you don't monitor your exertion. The "talk test" works just as well for cross-country skiing as running, especially for the longer training sessions.

Train by skiing

Canadian national ski coaches Jack Sasseville and

47

Anton Scheier, writing in *The National Guide to Loppet Skiing*, say, "Make your easy days easy enough so you can go hard on your hard days and make your hard days hard enough so you have to go easy on your easy days." Got it?

Running During the Winter

"Specificity" is a term that we hear frequently when reading about cross-country training or triathlons. There is a "use it or lose it" element to training that will cause most runners, even if they get serious about skiing, to continue some running all winter long.

Noted orthopedic surgeon Stan James, who excels in running and skiing at the masters level, believes that "While cross-country skiing in the winter will provide great cardiovascular fitness and great total body strength for the runner, the primary training mode must be running."

Keep running all winter

Hal Higdon, another great Masters runner who loves to ski, is also a believer in specific training. He says, "If you want to run better, you run. It's that simple."

Most experts believe that you should run at least once or twice a week during the winter. If you run several times each week, make it a moderate workout. Forget speed work and very long distance. You will find that skiing has your lungs and upper body raring to go, but your legs will have lost some of the running strength. I notice it after about five miles or so — the knees feel a little tight and the calf muscles get tired.

Former U.S. Nordic coach Mike Gallagher put it like this in an article: "Runners have to maintain contact with their running. Otherwise, you lose your running rhythms and running coordination, not to mention the loss of strength and fitness in specific muscle groups which don't exactly apply to skiing."

One good way to put some zing into your running workouts is to enter a couple of winter races — the "frostbite specials" or Super Bowl fun runs that are low key and frequented by the gung-ho of the running community. Just take it easy, remember that your running muscles are on a winter break. Winter relay races, where you can either run or ski — or if you are brave, skate or snowshoe — are quite widespread. If you are inclined toward triathlons,

Take it easy if you run a winter road race

there are a growing number featuring running, skiing, and snowshoeing.

The great thing about cross-country skiing is that it is an alternative, not an addition, to running. It allows you to back off and let the nagging little running injuries heal while you stay in good aerobic shape and maintain your weight. Don't defeat the purpose by overdoing it on the roads. Once or twice a week is fine. If you are getting itchy, back off the skiing and ease back into running. Find the balance that fits your body and the winter conditions around you.

4. Up and running on skis

Cross country skiing can, at first, be frustrating to aerobically-fit runners who, having read about what a great cardiovascular workout skiing is, give it a a try and then have a hard time remaining upright. Skiing, while quite easy at the basic recreational level, takes some practice and technique to get the kind of workout you get from running. Yet it doesn't take long to get proficient. Here's how to get started and how to get better.

Runners are, in most part, self-taught and self-coached. We read articles on training, talk to friends, and then just go out and run. Sometimes it takes advice from others to change our style of running. I learned that a while back after a local road race with my sons and some of their friends. "Boy, Mr. M.," one of the kids said, "you sure have a short stride for someone your size." My retort was of course, "Well, it's long enough to keep up with you," but it got me thinking — and gave me something to work on while running. This kind of feedback becomes even more important in skiing.

Get some feedback

Technique plays a much bigger role in cross country

skiing than in running. It pays to get some instruction early in the game. It is not just a matter of "looking good," it is more a matter of getting the most out of your effort. Without good technique, the good aerobic conditioning that you may bring from running is wasted. With good technique, you not only get a great workout, you feel so much better about it. Things are clicking, you're moving smartly on skis, and getting addicted to skiing. Many cross country ski racers, both elite and recreational, once were runners or cyclists. Now, instead of looking at skiing as something to do when it is too sloppy to run, they now run in order to get in shape to ski. Be careful, it could happen to you.

One of the reasons that cross country skiing grew so rapidly in the 1970s was the dictum, "If you can walk, you can ski." That saying helped sell a lot of skis and got a lot of people skiing — at a walking pace. But most runners want a higher level of action, comparable to their running. In other words, if you jog at a nine minute per mile pace, you'll probably want to ski at a similar level. On the other hand, if you are a speedster on the roads, you'll want to move out on your skis as well. In either case, it won't happen overnight, but with a little practice, it won't take too long. You're already conditioned, now all you have to do is learn to balance on skinny skis.

What about lessons? It is not a bad idea if you have qualified skiers available to teach you, but that's not always the case. Read the following pages, find some snow, and give it a try. You can get by for a while on the fact that

Use your "motor"

you've got a "good motor" and make up for a lot of inefficiency with your endurance base. One runner told me about his start in ski racing: "When I first started racing, I just went out and puffed and panted with the rest of them — it worked ok for a while."

Whether you take lessons at the start or wait until later, find an instructor who races. The person should be competent in all skiing techniques, including skating. Members of the Professional Ski Instructors Association (PSIA), if available in your area, should know how to get a runner up and running on skis. You'll find that instructors are too often saddled with out-of-shape beginners and should be eager to work with a motivated runner. Many instructors I know use video for feedback — a few hours spent with a pro will make your training time that much more efficient.

Group lessons are an inexpensive way to learn the basics

But let's face it, there is only so much time available to ski — weekends and an occasional evening will be it for most runners. So you may opt to just do your homework and get out and do it. Read up on technique, watch a couple of the videos listed in the back of this book, and get out and give it a try. (Some ski shops have videos that can be viewed in the shop or rented for a nominal fee.) Try to ski with someone who can help you. One of the best ways to learn is to trail behind a good skier, mimicking the moves, stride for stride, and seeing how it feels to do things right. Many coaches and good skiers have a good eye for technique so ask them to watch you. A couple of tips can go a long way toward smoothing out your skiing. Another trick some skiers use is to watch their shadow on a sunny day and see if they are skiing correctly. But as with any new sport, it is easy, as a friend of mine says, to get "paralysis by analysis." Don't over-analyze your skiing; concentrate on one or two things at a time and relax. If you keep your arms and legs flexed and your hips loose as you ski along, you'll be well on your way to efficient skiing technique.

Check out some of the ski videos

53

Diagonal Stride

Whether you teach yourself or go out with an instructor or coach, one of the first techniques, the "bread and butter" technique, that you will want to work on is the diagonal stride. This is the traditional method of cross country skiing, the classic image of the skier with ski pole planted in the snow, gliding with one leg suspended behind.

Striding is a lot like running

Fortunately for us, diagonal striding is a lot like running. But it is also deceptively difficult to perform well, so it may be years before we look like the skiers in the glossy photos. That's the look of a highly trained athlete with excellent balance — we have a ways to go yet.

Conjure up an image of how you might run on a day when the roads are covered with wet leaves or when there's a little freezing rain glazing the streets. Remember how carefully you planted each foot and got the weight shifted onto it? That pressing down feeling was what skiers call the "kick", the planting of the wax or the no-wax section of the ski to allow a pushoff. (The term "kick" is a misnomer; it really is more of a firm pushoff.) Keep that image of a slippery road in mind — we will use it as we head on out with the diagonal stride.

First, let's get the equipment on correctly. Most new binding systems do not have a "right" or "left" so your skis should fit on either side. Get the snow off the boot bottom and attach the ski. (On old 3-pin bindings, there definitely is a right and left so make sure that your heel is over the ski when the binding is snapped on.) Learn how to put the ski pole on by sliding your hand up through the strap. This allows you to put pressure on the strap when poling. There is also a right and a left for most good ski poles. Now you're ready to go.

Practice on a level area

Start on a level area. If you have a set of tracks to ski in, fine, otherwise just make some by walking with your skis in a straight line. Let your arms swing naturally just as you do when running. Just try walking on skis for a bit and once you are comfortable, try a little jog or shuffle, leaning forward just a bit. When you need to turn around, just move the ski tips, one at a time, like the hands of a clock, back to the reverse direction. Don't worry about your poles, just move your arms normally, keeping the poles headed slightly backwards.

With the example of running on a slippery road in mind, try jogging a little on your skis. Push off with one foot and drive the other leg forward. Shift your weight to that forward foot and glide on the ski that you have your weight on. This glide is the key to the diagonal stride. With your weight on the gliding ski and your knee bent, push down a little more, with pressure on your heel, (this is the racer's kick) and bring the other ski ahead. As you press that ski to the snow, the camber of the ski is flattened, allowing the wax or pattern on the bottom of the ski to do its thing — giving you the "grip" to push off. Keep the strides short at first. Get a little rhythm going, alternately pushing and gliding. It is a lot like running on skis, with a short pause for a glide. **Ride the glide**

The diagonal stride feels unusual at first because there is no "oomph" to it like in running. When you bring your foot forward you don't get that satisfying clump of a waffle-tread on asphalt. (Of course, that's why your running injuries tend to heal during ski season.) As mentioned before, when you push off or "kick", you want pressure on your heel, not the ball of your foot. You don't lift the foot, you just slide it, so at first it doesn't seem like as much of a workout. However, if you check your pulse, you'll find that you are exercising as vigorously as when you run, if not more.

Many runners who are just beginning to ski tend to be impatient and take shorter, choppier strides than more experienced skiers. This is caused by balance problems. It takes some time to learn to balance on a single ski so we tend to bring the other ski forward too soon, cutting off the glide. Try to think "glide" and let it flow but don't try to extend the glide artificially. Make a firm commitment of weight onto the gliding ski and swing your arms just as when you run. Get in the habit of planting the ski pole as soon as your hand comes forward. **Learn when to plant the pole**

As you ski, you'll lose the rhythm every so often and get out of synch with your skis. One common problem is to have your weight behind the lead (forward) ski which results in a "slap" as the ski comes down hard on the track. Practicing the stride on a slight uphill section of track will slow you down and help get your weight shifted to the forward ski. As your balance improves, you will get up over the front ski more and smooth things out. (For a very detailed analysis of the do's and don'ts of diagonal stride, see Lee Borowski's book listed in the Resource section.)

Plant the ski pole as soon as your arm swings forward

There are several practice techniques that can help you perfect the diagonal stride — one of the best is to ski without poles. So put your ski poles down and give it a try. You may feel a little unsteady at first, but concentrate on swinging your arms, just like a fast walk, and get the rhythm going. Don't forget to push off from the heel and transfer your weight to the gliding ski. Exaggerate the arm swing and see how easy it is to get moving right along. As you swing your arms faster, and rotate the body to transfer your weight, your speed will pick up. This drill is not just for beginners — I have seen elite skiers practicing without

Practice without poles

poles in tracks at many training centers. Try it a few times and then try using your poles. (As you will see, skiing without poles is also an excellent drill for skating on skis.)

Another drill that some ski instructors use is to have you ski on one ski: yes, that's *one* ski. Like riding a scooter, you push off with your ski boot and get the ski gliding. This exercise helps you learn to balance on one ski. It is a good way to make sure that you get out and over the moving ski and not be in a big hurry to jog along in a shuffling manner.

As soon as you can, start using the ski poles for more than just balancing. By now, you'll have noted that as you stride, your arms act just as in running — your right arm comes forward as your left foot comes forward. Hold your poles with the tips pointed backwards a bit (you can't get any power from poles that are straight up and down) and as soon as your arm comes forward, set the pole tip in the snow and give a little push. This is often called "planting" the pole. Keep your arms slightly bent, plant the pole in the snow and push as you drive past it with the other ski. Don't think too much about it, just be natural and let the poles come forward with your arm.

Be relaxed and pole naturally

Don't grip the pole handles too hard, it just tires the hands. Put the weight on the straps as you push, and as the pole goes behind you and your arm extends backwards, try to loosen the grip on the pole even more, until it is just between your thumb and forefinger. Experienced skiers release the grip on their poles altogether on the backswing.

Now that you have progressed from a basic jog/shuffle to a smooth diagonal stride with a rhythmic press-glide and your poling is coming along, it is time to hum the theme from "Chariots of Fire" and think about smoothness and efficiency. Recall the last time you saw a world-class runner on television, clicking off sub-five minute miles throughout a marathon. Remember how his head didn't bob, his stride was straight down the road, there was no wasted effort. That efficiency is what we want on skis. We want to focus our efforts directly ahead without a lot of extra motion. That's when the diagonal stride is fluid and nearly effortless — and fast.

Double Poling

Double poling is a technique that you will use a lot, especially on slight downhills where you get going a little too fast for striding, or when you want a change of pace. Once you feel comfortable on skis, this technique is quite easy to learn and it is efficient for beginners as well as elite racers. Double poling is simply a matter of reaching ahead with both poles, planting them, and compressing the upper body, gliding, and then reaching out and doing it again. When you watch a good skier double pole, it looks as if they are hinged at the waist.

Compress the upper body while double poling

Start on a level area which either has set tracks or that is well packed. Line your skis up so that they are parallel, then bend forward slightly, reach ahead with flexed arms and plant the ski poles in the snow with the pole tips angled slightly back. Keep the arms bent and lean toward the poles as you compress your upper body toward a horizontal position. You will be pulling on the ski pole straps initially and then, as you move between the poles, be pushing on them. Use your whole upper body: the trunk muscles, then the shoulders, finally the arms. Continue to let your arms follow through to the rear as your body bends and you'll be gliding. Reach forward and try it again.

Crunch the upper body

The faster you pole, the quicker you'll go. Compress the upper body to give power to the double pole. Your chest should come forward and your hips a little to the rear as you compress. Watch other skiers — notice how their arms and back stay at about the same angle as they double pole — they are "crunching" with the strong muscles of the upper body. (Some skiers practice by wearing their water bottle in front, so that they can "crunch" over it.) Runners often find double poling a lot of work because of the demands on the upper body. This is why cross country ski racers double pole all autumn on roller skis — to train the torso for double poling once snow comes.

The more advanced version of double poling combines the diagonal stride with the double pole and thus is called, the "kick, double pole." This powerful technique is used a lot by skiers on flat areas and on shallow downhills — times that you aren't going quite fast enough to double pole. Start with your hands at your sides and swing them forward together as you push off or "kick" one leg backwards. The trick is to kick just as your hands start forward. Then you compress over the poles, usually not as far as with a regular double pole, and after the glide, swing your arms out as you kick again. Most skiers switch legs each cycle, kicking off one leg and then the other. The timing of the kick, double pole takes some getting used to, but it can be a powerful tool in a runner's bag of ski tricks.

Master the kick, double pole

Most runners will find the double pole quite easy but the diagonal stride and the kick, double pole more difficult because they require more balancing on one ski. But before long, you can get feeling fairly confident on the flats. But the real fun in skiing lies over in yonder hills and dales. Now that we know how to get over there, we are ready for some hill work.

Climbs

Before getting up or down the hill, it might help to think about how to fall and how to get up from a fall. All skiers fall, even the best, so while falling has sometimes been associated with failure, it's really part of the routine for most runner/skiers. Knowing how to fall is important — to be loose and to sit down if you feel yourself going down. The more you ski, the less concerned you will be — it is no big deal so don't let it be. (My two worst falls in recent years were awful only because each time I fell on a fragile ski pole

Learn to fall

and snapped it. It wasn't my pride, it was my pocketbook that was hurt.)

Learn how to get up from a fall

Getting up from a spill can be tricky at first. If you are on a hill, swing your skis so that both are pointed across the hill (neither uphill nor downhill). Now, scrunch up and get onto your knees. Next, push yourself up with your hands, pushing on the skis. Your poles may be more of a problem than a help so take them off if they are in the way. Take your time. If things are really tangled, take off one ski and get vertical, then put the ski back on. Friends can be a big help — a helping hand saves a lot of effort when you are flat on your back and getting silly at your predicament.

Now to the hill. Runners who have not skied tend to hate hills at first. On the other hand, skiers with alpine experience can't wait to get up the hill so that they can bomb down the other side. Hills add an element of anticipation and a rush of adrenalin that runners don't often get — except when a German Shepherd makes a run at your flanks. Once you learn to handle hills, you can put your aerobic fitness to work on the climb side and get a nice rest on the downhill side. Instead of pounding down the hill on tired legs, you can grab a breather and glide down the slope. But first you need to get to the top.

Find an easy slope with a flat area on the top and a long runout area at the bottom. You can use the diagonal stride to climb some shallow hills. In racing, it is called "running the hill." Just as in running, gear down and use shorter strides as you start climbing and, keeping your weight forward, bound more, using good weight shift. Use your poles aggressively to help you and don't forget to compress (bend at the waist). If your skis start to slip due to the steepness of the slope, you will want to change to the primary climbing technique, the herringbone.

Run up shallow hills

Herringbone
Ever noticed "crow's feet" tracks up the side of a snowy hill? That's the mark of the herringbone. On steeper slopes, skiers get more grip by spreading the ski tips apart and keeping the tails together, forming the letter "V." Bringing the knees towards each other slightly, roll the skis so that the inside edges dig into the snow. That gives the grip. Continue to stride as before — walking or jogging up the hill with ski tips spread. You step up the hill or, in the case of racers, hop up the hill. Use the poles alternately, just as with the stride. Keep the poles in close to the body for more power. (Unlike the skier in the photo below.)

61

On easy hills, skiers normally climb using the diagonal stride and then shift to a herringbone as the skis start to slip. You can use a fairly narrow herringbone on shallow hills but as the hill steepens, the tips must become more open. Keep looking up the hill and make a good weight transfer from ski to ski.

The herringbone can be a good workout — it is easy to go into oxygen debt as you climb rapidly. As in running, keep your body forward and low to the ground and look up the hill. Shorten up the strides and try to keep your momentum up. You will use herringbone a lot: for touring, especially if you get into untracked terrain, and to conquer the hills that you'll find on most citizen racing courses. One of the unforgettable experiences in racing is to arrive at a big hill in the middle of the race, about the tenth skier in line, with each of you chugging up the hill until someone steps on someone else's pole, a skier falls, and the route is blocked. You spread your ski tips even wider, plant your poles, and stand there and pant. That's the herringbone.

Descents

Downhills put the spice in cross country skiing. You can really get moving on those skinny fiberglass skis strapped to your feet. Skiing fast down the hills makes the climbing work much more bearable. But first, one must learn ways to keep the speed and the thrills under control.

If you have found a gentle slope to climb, why not try skiing back down? Start with your feet a little wide and your legs flexed — this will let you use your legs as shock absorbers. Try a few easy downhills, bending your knees to ride over any bumps. You don't have to ski straight down the hill. Try traversing the hill, skiing nearly parallel to the fall line (an imaginary line straight down the hill), keeping most of your weight on the downhill ski. That's how you'll handle some of the steep slopes later on.

Use flexed legs to absorb the bumps

This is a good time to practice falling. As mentioned, smart skiers learn to sit down under control, sometimes called "bailing out," before they lose it altogether. Try it a few times, putting down your hands first and sitting down, then leaning off to the side. Remember to keep your skis across the hill as you get back up and use your poles to hold you in place until you are ready to go again. Don't start down until you are loose and ready.

Downhill skiing on cross country skis is why we climbed the hill in the first place — it is a great chance to catch your breath and enjoy the countryside. As you become more confident, you will look forward to nice speedy descents. But, before the countryside gets going by too fast, let's learn some ways to slow those skinny skis down.

Snowplow

There are many innovative ways of slowing down. We have just mentioned "bailing out" and there's also "drag both poles" or for real crises, "grab a tree." But for most situations, the best way to maintain speed is the good old snowplow.

Known also as the wedge, the snowplow is essentially the opposite of the herringbone — an inverted "V." To try it, start with a little speed and then, with knees bent slightly, push your heels outward, rolling the skis so that the inner edges dig into the snow. The tips should be nearly together and the tails spread wide apart, and you should feel some pressure in your quadriceps as you apply pressure to slow down. Try it a few times on a shallow hill, pushing out with the heels, slowing to nearly a stop, and then relaxing the pressure and continuing down the hill. Just as in the herringbone, the steeper the hill, the wider the "V" you'll make with the skis. Fool around with the snowplow until you are confident that you can keep your speed under control. If you put more pressure on one ski, what happens? You turned slightly, right? You just learned the snowplow turn.

Learn to snowplow early on

Turns

Snowplow Turn

Now that you have made a snowplow turn, let's work on it. Again, it is a matter of applying more pressure on one ski, digging the ski in, to turn in the opposite direction. Use your hands and ski poles to help "steer" into the turn, twisting the body slightly in the direction you want to go. Use the inner edge of the outside ski to dig in. Feel the pressure needed to turn? Back off the pressure and you

Weight the outside ski

are right back in the basic snowplow.

Try one to the left. Push out with the right heel, keeping your hands in front of you, and shift your weight onto that right ski. Your weight is on the ski that is carving the turn. Practice turning left and then right. Snowplow turns, while elementary, are the basis of most turning you'll do. Some runners may decide that they need not master any other turns; the snowplow turn will do it for them.

Step Turn

At slow speeds, changing direction using a step turn is fairly easy — it is same way we might turn while walking or running. The trick is to start with the inside ski, the ski on the side to which you are turning.

Try a turn to the right. Take a small step with the right ski and then shift your weight to that ski. Then bring the left ski tip up and over to match it. That's all there is to it. Make a series of small incremental changes. Practice on the flat as you work on your double poling and diagonal stride. At the end of the straightaway, turn using a series of step turns.

"Step" the turn

The step turn is used in a number of situations. It is especially helpful when traversing a hill to control speed. As you ski diagonally across the slope, you step up the slope a bit to slow down or if feeling brave, do a little step turn downward to pick up speed.

Skate Turn

There are times when a step turn, or even a quick series of them, won't get the job done, especially during a ski race. To negotiate a sharp curve and keep the speed up, you may need a step turn with a little more power; you may need a skate turn. (Next chapter will cover skating on skis in detail.)

First of all, you need a little speed to do a skate turn. Instead of stepping with the inside ski, push off the outside ski. You'll be skating off the inside edge of the outside ski. Try a right turn. With speed, skate off the left ski as you bring the right ski ahead. The rest of the turn is just like a step turn as you transfer your weight to the right ski and bring the left one up toward it. You then can skate off again if there's more turning to do. Racers take corners with a series of quick skates and actually can come out of the turn going faster than when they entered.

Advanced Turns

Runners are not known for caring too much about stylistic skiing. There are, however, some maneuvers that can make you a better skier on the downhills. Advanced versions of the snowplow turn are called the stem turn or the stem christie. These turns start with a half snowplow with the outside ski in the snowplow. Then, bearing down with the inside edge, you bring the inside ski parallel to the outside ski. Get an instructor to show you these to help you master the basics. A couple of sessions at an alpine ski area can go a long way to refining these techniques.

Try a few downhill lessons

Another turning method that became popular again in the 1980s was the telemark turn. Ever watched ski jumpers land, knees flexed, one ski ahead of the other? That is the telemark position. These graceful sweeping turns that work best with special skis and powder snow are popular with skiers who come from an alpine background. Most runners, interested more in cross country as an aerobic supplement, will tend to stick with the more conventional turning methods. There are numerous articles and books on the telemark technique.

We have looked at ways to ski on the straight and level, how to climb, descend, and turn. These basics, coupled with your runner's endurance base, will allow you to ski on prepared trails, to race in citizen races, or to bushwhack through two feet deep untracked snow in the wilds of Minnesota. Now we will look at skating, the fastest technique on cross country skis.

5. Skating on skis

Cross country skiing changed dramatically in the 1980s with the advent of the skating technique, which, at least for ski racing, revolutionized the sport. Performance-oriented skiers across the world, looking for more speed, changed their skiing ways and did it over the groans of traditionalists who felt that skating would ruin the sport. Now, when you visit nearly any nordic ski center, you will see some skiers using traditional techniques while others skate on glide-waxed skis. Skating is easy to learn and the fastest way to travel on cross country skis. It is something that many runners are going to want to master.

A new way to ski

The skating "revolution" was triggered by the "Johnny Appleseed" of U.S. nordic skiing, Bill Koch, who had earlier, with his silver medal at the 1976 Olympics, helped to start the boom in cross country skiing in the United States. He learned the technique from a Swedish racer who passed him during a race in 1980. Koch followed along, mimicking the skating method and brought the new technique home to practice. And practice he did, two years later, he skated his way to four World Cup tour victories and went on that year to become the first U.S. skier to win the World Cup. His accomplishments sent racers scrambling to learn the technique and changed the racing scene forever.

Racers scrambled to learn how to skate

Skating: easy and fun

Is skating for runners? Don't believe tales about how strenuous or demanding skating on snow is. They are misleading. Any fit individual, with some help on technique and equipment, can be up and skating on skis the first time out. Skating not only adds zest to cross country skiing for racers and tourers alike, it actually takes less energy once you master the technique. All over the snowy parts of the world, skiers from five to eighty are getting out and leaving "crow's feet" tracks across the countryside. Runners who want to ski for an aerobic workout will find that ski-skating is a nice addition to their "bag of tricks."

Runners who come to the sport of cross country skiing without the baggage of years of diagonal stride experience find skating easy to learn. The legs play a very big role in skating, and contrary to early opinions, one does not have to have the upper body of a gorilla to be a fast skater. And since skating, as we shall see, requires a full transfer of weight to the gliding ski, it can help your diagonal stride technique as well. Skating helps to correct the tendency of many runners to cut off their glide too soon.

Whether we race or not, there are several practical reasons for runners to learn to skate. Many of us don't have a lot of time to exercise — it's lace up the shoes, do a few quick stretches, and out the door we go for a run either before or after work. Skating can allow some of the same spontaneity if you have a place to ski-skate. The skis are ready and you can hit the golf course, the school grounds, or local snowmobile trails for a quick workout. Your chances to find a place to skate are usually better than finding a place with tracks to diagonal stride. **Get out and go**

You also are freed from the uncertainties of snow and temperature conditions. This can be important in changing weather conditions when wax or patterned bottoms just don't work. Skating, since it does not rely on grip, allows the runner a chance to get a good workout in virtually all snow conditions. For optimum enjoyment, learn both traditional and skating — then you can match your technique with the conditions and the amount of time you have available.

Getting Started

Once snow comes, runners have countless places to work on their skiing — the local golf course, town parks, county trail systems, or the nearest touring center. You can go out and diagonal stride in some conditions, cutting your own tracks, and then skiing in them. For skating, there are even more options but you need packed snow conditions. So to get started, find a place that is smooth and packed — either a wide snowmobile track or a cross country ski center.

As covered in Chapter 2, skating requires skis that have smooth bottoms and which are waxed with glide wax from tip to tail. The "no-wax" bottoms that work so well for diagonal stride make skating nearly impossible. The same goes for grip-waxed skis. The glide is reduced due to drag because the grip surface grips the snow as soon as you transfer your weight to the skating ski. If you've been skiing on waxable skis, scrape off the grip wax. You'll want **Skate on glide-waxed skis** some glider wax from tip to tail. Learn to skate on glide-waxed skis.

The key to skating, as with diagonal stride, is to get comfortable balancing on one ski and transferring your weight from one ski to the other. At first, beginners have enough trouble staying up on two skis, but with practice, you'll be able to relax and glide on one ski at a time. One **Learn to** good way to work on this, as we did practicing diagonal **transfer** stride, is to ski without poles. Start on an open flat area. **weight** Spread your skis into a slightly open position like a herringbone and edging the inside edge of your left ski slightly, step onto the angled right ski. With legs flexed, glide for a moment on the flat ski and then step back to the angled left ski. Don't worry about a lot of glide at first, stay loose and stay at it. The goal is to transfer your weight in a correct position — upright and gliding on the ski — and then thrust off onto the other ski.

When you step out onto a ski, turn your body in the direction the ski will be traveling. The body should follow the eyes — look in the direction the ski will be traveling. As you glide on a flat ski, your hips should be forward and your chin right over the gliding leg. Imagine that you have a crease in your ski pants. You should be able to look right down the crease from knee to ski. Some instructors call **Balance** this the "Toe-Knee-Nose" lineup. **over the**
ski As the glide slows, transfer your weight by rolling on the inside edge of the ski and pushing. At the same time, come powerfully off the ski into a balanced position on the other ski. Keep it fluid, and don't over-analyze the maneuver. It's really easy — kids pick it up with ease.

Here are some tips for better skating:

1. Don't rush; ride the glide. Balance is the key #1 to skating.

2. Work on developing a powerful leg push that comes from a quick bending and straightening of the hip, knees, and upper body. Weight transfer is key #2.

3. Bring your boot in next to the ankle of the gliding leg just prior to the next skate.

4. Remember that a flat ski is a fast ski and that you only want to edge the ski when you are ready to pushoff. It is a gradual process from flat ski to edged ski.

70

V-1 or 2 Skate (Double-Pole On One Side)

Once we get ski poles involved to help extend our glide in skating, we immediately get hung up with the terminology of skating techniques. Suffice it to say that V-1, also called the "2 Skate" (since you skate twice for every one double pole) is the generic skate technique that you will use most of the time. It simply combines the powerful skate that we've worked on with the legs with a good double pole. You pole and skate on one side and then skate, without poling, on the other side. This technique is the "plain vanilla" skating variation for most skiers.

Why not start by skating onto the right ski? Push off the left ski and turn your body as you start the double pole. The right ski and your ski poles should hit the snow at the same time. As the poling push is finishing, edge the gliding right ski and, just as before without poles, skate onto the left ski. Glide on this ski, and then edge it and pole back to the right side, compressing your upper body over the poles and balancing on the gliding ski.

It is easy to get too technical while describing ski techniques, but it is important to think about your ski pole placement while climbing with the V-1. The pole on the so-called "strong side," the side you are poling on, is vertical

Plain vanilla skating

71

while the pole on the other side is angled out. This is very natural. So don't let the ski pole terms trip you up. Use your legs to give much of the skating power, and use the poles to keep the glide going. And remember the keys to skating — balance and weight transfer.

The pole on the "strong side" will be vertical while the other is angled out

Diagonal V-Skate

This is a skating herringbone that is used to climb steep hills or when a skier is too tired to do much else. It is a nice climbing technique for the average runner/skier but even World Cup skiers use it on steep climbs, literally dancing their way up the hill. The poling is just like that for diagonal stride — the left pole helps you skate onto the right ski and vice versa.

The way to climb To get started, find a packed hill to climb and start by doing a regular herringbone. Try to get a little glide on each ski by poling onto the ski with the opposite pole. Revert to the herringbone if you start getting bogged down. Don't kill yourself trying to skate uphills — get what glide you can but concentrate on skating the rolling uphills and downhills where the skating is easier.

Marathon Skate

Marathon skating, with one ski in the track, is the technique that started the skating revolution. It is essentially the V-1 skate with one ski gliding in the track. The technique works well on narrow courses where there's not enough room to V-skate or when a skier does not want to mangle pre-set tracks by skating across them. In racing, it is often used when the tracks are icy and therefore faster than the skating part of the trail.

The skate that started it all

Runners will welcome a change of pace after V-skating, a chance to get into a set of tracks and use the marathon skate or to double pole for a while. Marathon skating is often less demanding than other forms of skating. The muscles used are just different enough to provide a welcome relief. This is a technique that can come in handy during long tours and loppets.

Marathon skating is fast when the track is glazed

Let's give it a try. Practice in a level area with a prepared set of tracks and get a good glide going by double poling. Plan to skate off the right ski and leave the left ski in the track. As you are gliding down the track, lift the right ski up slightly, angling the tip outward about 45 degrees. Put the angled ski on the snow as you double pole in that direction. The angle will remain about 45 degrees throughout the glide phase. Transfer your weight to the angled right ski and balance. Don't be shy about committing to the skating ski — remember the "toe, knee, nose" alignment. As the glide ends, push off with the inner edge of the right ski, just as in V-skating, and shift your weight back to the left ski which should be gliding down the track. Balance on the tracking ski, bringing the right foot all the way back into the tracking foot (coaches call it "clicking your heels), then double pole onto your right ski and try it again. You can fly down the track with the marathon skate.

Click your heels

If you approach the marathon skate as just a variation of the generic V-skate, it is easy to master. Just remember to make a good weight transfer from ski to ski and balance on the gliding ski. Sound familiar?

Gunde Skate (V-2 Alternate)

Sometimes called the open field skate, this is a variation on the V-1 and is used on the flats and shallow hills and dales. This is a great technique to learn by skating behind a good skier since you need to get out on the gliding ski before poling, then skate in the opposite direction. You can really get moving because you keep the skis going straighter down the track and glide longer on each ski. Popularized by Sweden's great Gunde Svan, this technique requires good balance.

V-2 (One Skate)

This is a technique for racers or for when you want to look like one. It is very fast, very demanding, and very difficult for average skiers. Basically, it requires a double pole on each glide. It is a good drill because it requires excellent balance and forces you to commit to a gliding ski, then recover and commit to the other. Most runners won't waste their energy doing it.

Experts like V-2

74

Skate behind good skiers and mimic their moves

Free Skating (Skating Without Using Poles)

This is a racing technique which is used for quick downhills that are too fast for poling. It is also used on the flats to rest the arms. Skiers skate with their bodies in a low aerodynamic position while swinging their arms and their poles from side to side much as a speed skater. As you develop your skating, try mixing in some free skating from time to time — it is a good way to work on weight transfer and balance. And it's not that difficult.

Equipment For Skating

A generation of skating skis, bindings, and boots has been developed since the skating phenomena hit cross country skiing. Skating skis are single-purpose skis with one ambition in life: to skate fast on a packed surface. They look fast as well, featuring flashy graphics and brilliant paint jobs. It is easier to skate on these special skis but because they lack a wax pocket, they are unsuited for the traditional techniques. So racers need at least two pairs of skis. For runners entering the sport, any good light touring ski can be used for skating and as mentioned in Chapter 2, there are a number of good "combi" skis on the market. These allow both skating and diagonal stride.

To skate, you will want a shorter ski and a stiff boot with

Flash and dash

good ankle support. Again, a dual-purpose boot that allows both techniques is probably your best bet. The most important purchase for skating will be your ski poles. It is essential to have poles long enough and stiff enough. Long poles allow you to get up and over your skis and apply the poling force through much of the glide. Skating poles should be about chin high although many skiers use poles that are about nose high. Spend enough to get poles that will not flex excessively when you use them. For that, you'll have to pay at least $50.

Skate with long poles

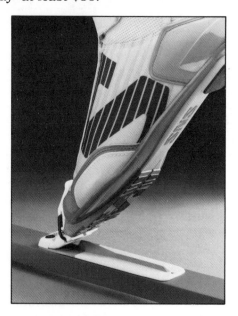

A new generation of ski boots was designed for skating

While you can skate on virtually any set of cross country equipment, runners who decide to get serious about this fast new way to travel on snow will want to consider buying skating gear. The new gear is flashy and fast and fun, not unlike a sports car. The boots will give you firm support throughout the glide and pushoff, the skis will provide a stable yet quick platform to balance on, and the poles will help power you along. Yet, just like a sports car, when the snow is new and piled high, keep them in the garage.

Skating and Running — Problems?

Skating on skis uses muscles in the thighs that you don't use in running; you direct pressure straight down the inside of the leg to the ski. After your first day of skating, you may feel it in the abductor muscles. You also may have sore arms and shoulders, especially if you skate with long poles.

You may have some sore arms and shoulders after using long poles for skating

You can do some specific training for skating before the season to tone up your skating muscles. Serious racers practice skating on roller skis or training skates. Another system that some racers use is the slideboard — a system borrowed from speed skaters. Slideboards are simply a six to eight foot sheet of formica counter top (look in your discount lumber houses or talk to contractors who renovate kitchens) with padded sidewalls. Slide some wool socks over your shoes and you are in business. Push off with one leg, just as in skating, and slide to the opposite side of the board on your other foot.

Runners may find it easier to train for skating by modifying their running a bit. When you go out with poles to run hills in the fall, instead of charging straight up the hills, run diagonally back and forth across the slopes, bounding off the inner muscles. This tends to look and feel

Train by running

77

a bit awkward but it is good specific training for skating. You can also work on the double pole by striding and double poling once every three strides. I count to myself, "One, two, three, pole," as I motor along.

Bound off the inner leg muscles as you run

Skating will pose a dilemma for some runners. Do we really want to develop muscles that might be antagonistic to running? For most runners who run to stay in shape and perhaps pick up some age group ribbons, it won't be a big thing. The aerobic training and the fun of skating on skis outweighs a few potential "de-training" items that can be straightened out in the spring.

Skating has been around long enough to develop some patterns. There have been the typical overuse injuries at the elite level but no serious side effects noted in the ski literature that would concern recreational runners. My running friends who skate do well in their spring races and have noted no problems. Most of us try to take a couple of runs each week during ski season to let the running muscles know that they've got work ahead next season.

The one concern that has surfaced is one that could effect runners. Some athletes and physiologists feel that skating, especially at the elite level, may not be as good an aerobic workout as diagonal stride. Try to tell this to a struggling beginner, hunched over his skis, trying to skate up a hill. But that may very well be the reason — skating produces more lactic acid, probably because more muscles come into play, and consequently may keep you anaerobic too long. Regardless of the reasons why, it is no secret that most serious skiers combine both traditional and skating in their training to make sure that they stay in top shape.

Mix classical and skating

Skating, once learned, is a fun workout. It is a little like getting up on water skis for the first time — once you get the picture and the feeling of balance and thrust locked in your mind, then it's just a matter of working on it and gaining experience. But don't get too analytical — there are reams of technical articles written on the fine points of skating. Yet, if you just jump in and stay relaxed and do it, you'll learn your personal way to skate and tailor it for the conditions you encounter. I like skating for training reasons. Without a lot of worry about snow temperatures, I can be out the door and on my skating skis in minutes. After a 45-minute workout of V-skating around a nearby field (snowmobile tracks work quite well), I come back dripping wet and tired, just as at the end of a good run. That's why I skate.

Relax and have fun

Young skiers find skating easy and fun

6. Let's race

I had just shed my jacket and sweat-soaked polypropylene top when, with a swirl of snow and wind, my friend Bob crawled into the car. The windows steamed up as we both struggled into dry clothes, clothes that had been sitting in the cold car for hours. As we munched on orange slices, drank from water bottles, and waited for the car to warm up, he said, "You know, some folks would think that we're nuts. But it's great, isn't it?" Most of the 300 skiers who, like us, had just completed the 15K cross-country race on that cold, windy Saturday would have agreed. Some had driven five hours or more just to get there. They, like us, had caught the fever of nordic racing.

Cross-country ski racing is like running was back in the 1970s. Each season brings more events and more skiers giving local races a try. No longer for just a few devotees, nordic racing has gained attention and participants. In fact, while road racing has leveled and the number of runners in some races is dropping, nordic ski races, often called citizen races, are growing in number. There is a place for everyone in most races. Hot skiers can whizz off

Look for local ski races

at the front of the pack while their grandparents can take their time at the back. This mix of age and ability that makes so many local runs a family and social affair will likewise appeal to runner/skiers who decide to try a few citizen races.

There's a place for everyone in a citizen race

Whether you run a 10K race each weekend or just try a local "fun run" once a year, you can find a whole new competitive world in ski racing. You will find the same camaraderie and acceptance of newcomers that is prevalent in road racing. You also will find that there are new opportunities to win age group awards and to set new PRs.

Types of Races

There are two basic types of cross country races: the open race and the citizen race. The open races are aimed at the competitive skier and may be strictly for one particular age group, say junior skiers. Racers are categorized by the U.S. Ski Association into four broad categories: Bill Koch Ski League (9-13), Juniors (14-19), Seniors (20-29), and Masters (30+). Open races will usually feature an interval start, where two skiers head out every 30 seconds. It is the way many of the Olympic and World Cup nordic races are held. Most of the racers at open races will be classified members although it is usually possible for other skiers to participate.

Be wary of these open races — the stiff competition may not be suited for the novice racer. Don't be afraid to call the race organizer, explain your situation, and just ask if this is a race for you. If it looks like you'll be outclassed, try one of the citizen races around where you will fit into the pack better. However, open races offer a great chance to study good cross country skiers in action. It is fun to watch the ease with which they fly down the course and skate up the hills. It is a good chance for runners to find out exactly what techniques are being used by the top skiers. Find a race and watch it — you will be amazed at the skill and the speed of these athletes.

Watch a few elite races

Open races feature interval starts

Citizen ski racing is a lot like road racing was ten years ago. Many of the races are low key, with inexperienced organizers, and nothing goes quite as planned. Some runners find skiers more abrasive, more testy when the gun goes off. The conflict between skaters and diagonal striders can also trigger boorish behavior. Yet, the spirit among most racers is just like you will find at a local 10K on a Saturday morning. Many runners, once they get their skiing technique down, get hooked on citizen racing. It's a great workout and lots of fun.

Finding ski races is not always easy. I've asked at good ski shops about the upcoming races and got a blank look from the salesperson. You just don't find the piles of race applications around that you do for road racing — it is a much more closed operation, much more like bike racing in that respect. Even the ski magazines do not have race calendars. Check your ski shops, touring center, or local ski club, and ask your skiing friends.

In the U.S., a good source of information is the USSA. They put out a nordic competitor's manual that lists every race in your section of the country. The price, for a beginner, is pretty steep ($50.00) but for that, you become a classified racer, get into some races at reduced fees, and get a subscription to a ski racing newsletter. Why not borrow a manual from a racer the first year or so, then take the plunge and join up? In Canada, the provincial offices of Cross Country Canada can steer you to both ski clubs as well as races in your area.

Where to find races

There are other ways to find out what's coming up for races. Ski club newsletters often list local races, some of the non-sanctioned events that may not be on other schedules. Some clubs have race "hot lines" with recorded messages about upcoming events. One of the best ways to learn about future races is to ask other skiers after a race — you'll hear about some races you didn't know existed. For years, the ski race circuit was publicized by grapevine, and it still pays to be tied into a network. Then when an event is changed to the following week due to lack of snow, you won't be driving hours to get to a non-existent race.

Why Does Racing Cost So Much?

It pays, literally, to find out where and when the races are. If you are interested in entering an open race, you usually will have to pre-register because there is a cutoff date several days before the race. (The entries are set up for the interval starts ahead of time so there is usually no day-of-race registration.) Many mass start citizen races allow you to sign up on race day, but as in road racing, there is often a pretty stiff penalty. Unlike road racing, early registration is a gamble, especially if the season is marginal due to snow conditions. If you pay early, a January thaw may wipe out the race and along with it, your entry fee. But, if you wait, you pay more. This becomes even more critical in major marathon races where fees often double or triple as race day nears.

Register early

If you grumble over the escalating entry fees in road running, you will be even more unhappy over the prices of most ski races. While there are still a few $5 or $6 races around, most fees are high and you get nothing but a race — no T-shirts, biking caps, or even sweatbands. The larger races usually have finisher pins or medals but the entries are $25 or more.

Don't expect a T-shirt

Trail grooming is an expensive part of race course preparation

Putting on ski races is a costly business and one that usually falls to volunteer groups such as ski clubs. In addition to the costs associated with any race — publicity, entry forms, bibs, awards, and timing equipment — ski races also pay head taxes to the U. S. Ski Association for sanctioning and insurance and also often have major costs associated with trail grooming and track setting. You don't run Sno-Cats up and down a long course for nothing. Ski race management is a little more than painting arrows on the road, putting out a few cones, and getting the sheriff to help with traffic. It is an expensive undertaking and the entry fees reflect this.

Before The Race

Ski races, whether a local winter carnival race or a big name event attracting 500 skiers, have the same atmosphere that 10K road races do. But there's more to it than just lacing up a pair of flats and lining up so get there in plenty of time to get both yourself and your equipment ready to go. Race registration is often painfully slow and the hubbub is added to by racers trying to wax their skis, change into racing suits, or just stay warm before the race.

Give yourself time

If you have ever marveled at the pre-race nervous energy of runners — the exotic stretches, the yoga stances, the high-stepping sprints of the elite runners, you will love the atmosphere at citizen races. First are the outfits. Hot skiers wear hot clothing these days and skiers seem to try to outdo each other in ski finery as well as ski finesse. You have to be a good skier to wear a home-designed lycra Spiderman outfit. Yet, on the other end of the clothing spectrum, I've seen racers with wool plaid hunting coats (with the license still pinned on the back) and wooden skis. If you wear a wind suit or running tights, you will fit right in to the citizen racing scene.

Enjoy the pre-race hoopla

Watch good skiers wax before the race

The pre-race psychology is just as prevalent at ski races as at road races: the same stories about how little one has trained, the comments about being injured all add up to the same hype and white lies that add spice to friendly competition. But the thing that sets skiing apart is the waxing and ski tinkering that goes on. In one corner, a skier might be wrestling with a gooey tube of blue klister while nearby, a front runner sets up a portable waxing bench and opens up a box holding an array of wax that looks like an organic chemistry lab. I'm always reminded of the weekend bass fisherman and his four-tray tackle box with about 25 pounds of lures. He probably really only uses a couple of favorites. The same holds true for many skiers — especially skaters with trays of glide wax — they trust a couple of favorites and carry the rest as sort of a security blanket. If you look at their waxes, several will be nearly gone while most others are untouched. Watch good skiers wax before a race, you can learn a lot from them.They'll help you wax. The attitudes of cross country skiers toward newcomers is great. I have never felt as though I was invading a clique. People seem glad to share information about equipment, trouble spots on the race course — it is a very supportive atmosphere and a good reason to arrive early. Try to find out who the top skiers are and watch them warm up. I like to meet them and wish them well — you will find that they are very accessible and often very helpful.

Watch and learn

There's not as much stretching before ski races, mostly because there are few places to do it without freezing. It is important to warm up, check out the skis and the wax, and stay warm right up to the start. It is tough to find water ahead of time so bring your own and just as in running, hydrate before the race. Again, as in road racing, you will have to balance your intake versus outgo by judicious timing of visits to the latrines. It is a slow process with several layers and zippers to contend with.

Warm up

When you first race, it is difficult to figure out how much to wear out on the course. The tendency for beginners, as in road racing, is to wear too much and overheat. There are a couple of things to carry: a water bottle in a holder because you get really warm and lose a lot of fluids while racing, and a tiny wax bag with a light shell to take care of any sudden drops in temperature. With a hat and gloves, you should be comfortable. The slower you race, the more clothing you want to carry or wear. Many skiers who enter just a few races carry fanny packs with some clothes and some snacks to get them through the race. Take your lead from others. After a couple of races, you'll have the picture.

Dress for racing

The Start

If you like friendly chaos, you'll love mass starts at citizen races. Until you have raced a while, it will be a little hard to seed yourself, not knowing how fast you'll ski. If you have developed some skiing skills, don't start too far back in the pack because you will go nuts trying to pass slower skiers and to avoid general disaster. Look for people who appear to be the same caliber as you. Get in place and sort of spread out a bit, staking out a claim. You'll find that

Starts can be chaotic

Find a starting spot that fits your ability

good skiers will squeeze in at the head of the pack, but just like in road racing, there will be a few novices up too far front. That can be downright dangerous in ski racing — it's sometimes a melee of ski poles and skis during the first rush. Runners, used to road racing, will know that there's a lot of race ahead and that things will settle down as skiers find their own pace and niche.

Skating invites tangled skis and poles. Many races call for double poling during the first 100 yards or so and then the back and forthing starts. For new skiers, there's a real chance of entanglements and falls so keep alert, and when it happens, stay cool, get up and go. If you are kick waxing for diagonal stride, you will know by the first mile if your wax is right for the snow. Tracks often get glazed by the skiers ahead, and your skis may tend to slip more than you want as the race goes on. It might be smart to stop right there and correct things before wasting too much effort.

Skiing The Race

Racing protocol calls for passing on the left if there are two tracks and stepping aside if there is only one. There is a lot of passing, more than in running, during the first 5K of shorter races. Some skiers are better climbers than others, some better on the downhills, others seem to ski in spurts, speeding up and slowing down. Most skiers are polite, saying or yelling "Track" or "On your left" to let you know they are going by. In many races, there is a set of tracks for traditional and a skating lane. You can switch into the tracks and double pole if a faster skater needs to get by you. It is important not to rush when passing or being passed — the other skier can wait. This is no time to tangle and fall.

Pass on the left

Watch out for the first downhill because that can be where the falls and pileups start. One of the race courses that I ski each year has a tough downhill about 20 minutes into the race. For the middle of the pack racers, the race grinds to a halt at this point as skiers line up and wait their turn to "run the gauntlet." It is quite a sight the first time — skiers howl as they rip down the hill and then take a spill the bottom, trailing skiers madly maneuver to miss the down skiers, while others, probably smart runners, say, "Forget this," and take off their skis and jog down the hill. When you first start racing, you'll probably encounter a few situations like this. Don't worry, you can make up time on the flats and the climbs.

It is easy to get going too fast and lose control when descending at race speeds. It takes practice and leg muscles to hold a good snowplow on a steep downhill. You can really feel it in the quads as you press to keep the edges dug in. If you are in double tracks, use one ski in a snowplow for speed control. What happens to many nov-

Control speed on descents

ices is that they get tired, relax the snowplow, and start moving down the hill too fast. Be ready for icy, semi-bare downhills since many racers ahead of you have already dug in and scraped snow away. All the reason to get faster and further up in the pack next year. Before long, you'll welcome downhills as a nice breather.

Uphills, especially those early in the race, are also potential bottlenecks. The leaders glide right up the hills in a strong skate but further back, the pace slows. This can be a chance to catch your breath and relax even though you are climbing. The slow herringbone climbs are good places to use your running strength. What you lack in technique you may make up for in conditioning.

Hills can be bottlenecks during the race

As with downhills, the folks ahead of you can present problems on the uphills. Just as you switch from a skate or diagonal to a herringbone, a skier up ahead runs out of gas and the whole line stops, and starts, and stops. Keep at it, keep your weight forward, and as you crest the hill, try, as you might in running, to pass the skiers who are tired from the climb.

As the race goes on, you can expect to have the tracks pretty well chewed up by the racers ahead, especially when **Expect a** the course is narrow. Most races are set for skating on the **cut up** left and traditional technique on the right. Skaters try to **race** stay out of the tracks, unless they are marathon skating or **course** double poling, but the course tends to get really chewed up in certain conditions.

Watch good racers
and learn from them

Ski races are great places to get faster — it's a good chance to watch others and imitate them. Just as in road running, it pays to stay relaxed and try to be efficient. Even though it may be frigid weather, take fluids when you can. Many shorter races don't have feeding stations so carry your own. Drink water or a replacement fluid from your water bottle on the downhills. You can lose a lot of water in a ski race — studies have shown that elite skiers lose over three pounds of water in a 20K race and up to 13 pounds in a marathon. Some races have sweet drinks at stops. I'd stick with water if it is available — this is no time for dietary experimentation. In longer races, you'll need some energy replacement, either liquid or solid.

Replace fluids

As the race progresses, you may start to "bonk" a bit. The simplest downhill can present problems late in a race. Concentrate on technique and try to ski smoothly. As you approach the finish, forget the last minute sprints (runners know how "bush" that can be) because all you need is to spread-eagle ten yards from the finish. You will be tired, but if you've skied a smart race, not exhausted. You'll be surprised how quickly you recover.

Now's the time to get some fluids and food (the banana and oranges froze in the car but they're still tasty) and to get into something warm and dry. Few races have shower facilities but bring a towel and sweats and get something warm on right away. Before too many races, you will have learned new techniques for getting dressed and undressed in the car. Don't forget a dry hat as well. This is a good time to check on upcoming races and to do a few stretches. Get the ski gear put safely away and take a moment to think about things in the race that will help you ski an even better race next year. Because you will be back.

7. Let's tour

Long before cross country ski centers began to dot the countryside, skiers were enjoying the specialness of ski touring. This "do-it-yourself" aspect of nordic skiing draws thousands to the sport each year. It is a chance to shed some of the trappings of a regimented lifestyle, to get away from the telephone or the fax machine, and enjoy the winter outdoors — and get some exercise in the bargain.

Runners who learn to ski well may wish to get into ski racing, but others may opt for a break from the racing scene. Ski touring provides "participation" in place of "competition." Whether it is an outing on a nearby golf course, a few loops around the local ski touring center, or a day hike in the back woods, ski touring provides a leisurely workout for a runner. It provides the chance to enjoy the company of family and friends and the special world of winter. The stillness of a January morning — trees creaking in the sharp air — the pleasure of watching your ski tips plow through powder snow — the camaraderie of stopping on the trail for lunch — are some of the reasons that touring is so popular.

Take a break from racing

There are many cross country skiers who could care less about V-1 skating, Kevlar ski poles, lycra racing suits, or groomed trails and set tracks. That's not cross country skiing to them. Some, converts from the glitz of the alpine skiing scene, admire the simplicity and the low costs of ski touring. Others just like the fact that touring has none of the trappings of trendiness — it is a lot like walking or hiking — a chance to wear old clothes, go out when you want to, and stay as long as you want.

Touring lets you enjoy family and friends and the special world of winter

Runners have a chance to sample all sides of cross country skiing. Being in shape, they can jump into low-key citizen races and enjoy the opportunity to compete in a new sport. On the other hand, with the same set of skis, boots, and poles, they can "do their own thing" and never get near organized skiing and masses of skiers. Ski touring involves skiing at a moderate pace — more like walking than running. Heart rates, except in climbs or deep snow conditions, do not get elevated into the training zone. But does that matter? Carrying a small pack with a lunch and

An aerobic bargain

drinks, touring for hours at a time, feeling pleasantly tired at the end of the day, can provide as much mental conditioning as physical training. It is this flexibility that is attractive — you can go out and ski tour all day without paying an arm or a leg, or often, anything. It is one of the best aerobic bargains around.

Ski touring is a lot like walking

Where To Go

Runners just learning to cross country ski will find it easier to ski tour at facilities that have groomed trails and set tracks. Many of these sites not only have an extensive networks of trails, they also grade the trails according to difficulty. This way, a novice can concentrate on technique and enjoy the outing — with no need to be concerned about getting lost or about whether or not there is a killer hill around the next bend. While some nordic ski centers rival the alpine areas for glitter and costs, most are smaller family-run organizations which cater to the beginner. Even so, many ski tourers would rather shun the tracks and the other skiers, get away from the warming huts and groomed trails, and strike out on an adventure. It might be an outing with friends, skiing down an old logging road for a hot dog cookout or even a week-long expedition with full camping gear. For most runner/skiers, ski tours will be day trips — a "let's pack up and ski for a while" type of outing. You can do that nearly anywhere there is snow.

Try some local tours

Short local ski tours — the trip to the county or provincial park, the school grounds, or the snowmobile trail — are good chances to get experience for longer outings. You can learn what to take, how fast to ski to fit the pace of the group, and whether you even want to tackle more ambitious outings. The next step may be to try a tour on some rural farmland or woodlots, perhaps using some existing snowmobile trails. Don't assume that open land is "free" for skiing, even if it is not posted. Take some time to ask permission. There is nothing more maddening to a rural landowner, who has just received a staggering property tax bill in the January mail, than to see a carload of skiers pile out and troop out across the pasture without permission. Asking first is just common courtesy; most landowners don't mind having skiers using their land.

What To Wear

Ski touring is like touring on a bicycle — not a mad dash from point to point but rather a chance to cruise on skis, to observe and appreciate the winter scenery. The pace is steady enough to keep warm but not fast enough to cause one to break into a heavy sweat. Because of the more relaxed tempo, you need a little more clothing than you might for a concentrated ski workout.

As with any ski outing, dress in a number of light layers. Most ski tourers plan on three layers. First comes a layer of long underwear of one of the new materials such as polypropylene. These new fabrics tend to wick moisture away from your body so that you avoid that chilled, clammy feeling that comes from getting wet and then cold. Next comes a more insulating layer that is warm, especially on the upper body. This might be a light wool sweater or a turtleneck made of a material such as Polarfleece®. You will find that your legs will usually stay warm without an insulating layer. The outer layer, which might be carried in a pack if it is warming up, is a wind-proof, weather-repellent layer. Here is where a winter running suit top is great. Most skiers shy away from blue jeans which tend to chafe when the denim gets wet. Some touring skiers opt for a pair of long ski socks and knickers, short pants which come to just below the knee. These are very traditional and quite functional as well. Whether you want to buy them as opposed to a pair of running tights is a personal choice. I've collected a pair of both over the years. Two pairs of socks, usually a light poly sock under a wool sock, keep the feet warm and dry for touring. Lastly, a warm hat and mittens or gloves to warm the extremities and you are ready to roll. Protect your eyes from the sun with sunglasses or goggles and use a sunscreen.

Dress in layers

Don't dress too warmly for ski touring

97

Most beginners dress too warmly, get sweaty during the first climb, and then get chilled. It takes experience to find out what works for you, but if you've been running and walking during the winter months, you've already got a pretty good idea. I like to ski on the lightly dressed side, keeping my old nylon shell stuffed in my pack in case the weather changes.

What To Bring

Obviously, if you are only out for a tour in the local park, there is little else that you need. If you have kick wax skis, carry a couple of tins in your pocket (to keep the wax warm) and bring along a plastic scraper. Orange slices in a zip bag are easy to stow and if there is clean snow, taste great dipped in snow. I carry a water bottle in a holder for most any length tour.

For longer outings, you want to be better prepared, not only so that you can enjoy a lunch along the way, but so that you can deal with any unexpected problems. A fanny pack or small backpack is used to carry food and clothing. Here are some things that you might consider having along on any trip outside the local area (Throw the non-food items in a pack and just have them there for any outing):

What to carry

A pair of wool socks (great for cold hands as well)
A replacement ski tip (carry one and you'll never need it)
A small first aid kit
Swiss Army knife
A couple of screws for bindings
Compass and map
Candle, waterproof matches
Whistle
Extra clothing
Trail snacks (raisins, oranges, cheese & crackers)
Water bottle

Be ready

Reviewing this list, it looks as if we are going to trek across wilderness areas and use all our Boy Scout or Girl Scout survival skills along the way. Actually, ski touring is pretty tame, yet, anyone can get a little turned around. Ever been caught out on a long run by a sudden storm? You know how cold you can get and how scary the situation can become. On the ski trail, that 40 degree sunny day can plummet to a wind chill of 40 below when a cold front passes. Put the gear into a little sack, stow it in your fanny pack, and you'll probably never need it.

Bringing the kids along

It is smart to tour with others and not go out on your own. Before you start out, let someone know where you are going and how long you will be gone. Usually, three skiers is considered a minimum — then if someone twists an ankle, one can stay and one can ski out for help.

Day Trips

While one of the attraction of ski touring is its free-form nature, there are some things to keep in mind when you're going out all day. We already covered the items to go in the pack so let's review some other basics.

Planning — It is a good idea to check the route over beforehand with a topographical map, especially if you don't have someone along who knows the area. If you are not too sharp on reading contour lines, this pre-ski study **Study the** gives you a chance to learn or dust off map reading skills. **route** You can spot potential trouble areas — marshy spots that might not be frozen over, steep hills, or streams and rivers that might need to be crossed. If you are just going out in a neighbor's woodlot, you can obviously do without a map. But for backcountry skiing in unfamiliar terrain, a little homework with a U.S.G.S. topo map is a good investment.

Out and back trips are the most common. If there is new snow, you get to take advantage of the tracks you made on

the way in. On the other hand, looped tours let you explore new terrain all the way. One-way trips require some logistics planning — somehow you need to get a car positioned at your destination.

For many runners, ski touring planning will consist of, "It's a great day, let's load up the skis and go." With a few goodies to munch on, you are off on an outing. This spontaneity of touring is one of its charms. For many, it can be spoiled by too much planning.

Just load up and go

Hitting the Trail — Pick a safe place to park the car. While that might seem obvious, more than one skier's car has been buried by snowplows. Don't block farm roads or woods roads — remember that loggers and farmers work on weekends. Aim the car out of the wind so that you don't return to an engine compartment filled with snow. Check that the headlights are off and that you have a spare key.

Whether racing or touring, bridge crossings can be challenging

(Last winter, a good friend lost his car keys in a spill in the snow and had to leave the car — fortunately others were there to provide transportation.)

It is a good idea to leave food and drinks in the car. Water in a plastic water bottle won't freeze during most outings. High energy foods like brownies and cookies are great to come back to. You will have earned a decedent snack.

Bring spare keys

Setting the Pace — Tours are for fun, not for interval training, so don't be a "hyper" runner with too much energy. Most likely there's a mixed bag of athletic ability and conditioning along — so set the pace to keep everyone together. There's no point in trying to use a ski tour in place of a running workout — you will just get frustrated and also end up with some unhappy campers behind you. One solution is to get the aerobic workout with a quick run in the morning — or else just use the tour day as a rest day.

Touring can give you a pleasantly tired feeling at the end of the day but you won't have gotten much aerobic training. If you'd like, you can squeeze in a little extra work by carrying the heaviest pack, offering to break the trail for the gang, or by skiing up ahead to check out spots for lunch. Carrying a child on the back or pulling one behind in a "pulk" is another good way to get some extra training in. If you are leading the tour, be sensitive to the others' conditioning — not everyone likes to say, "Hey, slow down a bit, this isn't a forced march." Take some breaks for snacks or to admire a view and let everyone get their energy restored.

Don't force the pace

Along the Trail — Some of the most interesting parts of tours are the crossings — the streams, the fences, and the roads. If you are traversing a wet area, be alert for icing on your skis. Slide the skis forcefully along, trying not to lift them, wiping them clean on the drier snow after the crossing. Even so, you might check the bottoms. In half a minute you can scrape off any mud or ice and save lots of energy in the kilometers ahead.

Bridges likewise present some interesting challenges for the ski tourer. Many woods bridges are planked with slats and gaps just wide enough to catch a ski pole or even a ski. If the bridge looks too challenging, take your skis off and walk it. The same goes for fences. Barbed wire and P-Tex ski bases seem to have an affinity. If you have to cross fences, it may pay to take off your skis, even though you sink in the snow. Be careful because wood and barbed wire are brittle in the cold. Don't inadvertently snap a strand by standing on it.

Lunch on the Trail — Eating can be an ongoing activity while skiing — some raisins to nibble, some granola bars, some orange slices — all make the miles more enjoyable. It's a side of skiing that runners aren't used to, but it's an easy habit to pick up. You are burning those calories. Meals on a tour can be anything from the backpacker's GORP (good ol' raisins and peanuts) to a full-blown meat and potatoes meal. Most skiers, unless on a long tour with backpack gear, carry a light lunch and drinks. Sandwiches and a thermos of hot chocolate often fit the bill. Snack as you go

What about open fire cookouts? Picture a group of toasty-warm skiers, grouped around a campfire, warm food in their stomachs, smiles for one another? Right out of a ski magazine or a Miller Lite commercial, right? Now try picturing a smoldering collection of wet sticks, four raw hot dogs struggling to decide whether to freeze or thaw in the smoke, and several "getting colder by the minute" skiers wondering what idiot decided to stop and eat, and you've got another side of lunch along the ski trail. By all means, if you are experienced in the woods, find a sheltered spot, clear the snow away, and construct a fire to cook on. You may even want to bring some paper and dry kindling from home. Use the wood already down and dead and keep the size of the fire reasonable. Clean up the area and double check that the fire is extinguished before you depart the area.

Lunch on the trail can be fun

103

If you are serious about cookouts, a small propane stove such as those used in backpacking may be the best bet. It can heat liquids fast and is light and reliable. It gets the job done without all the smoke and sarcasm.

Drink plenty of liquids while touring. Even though you may not be perspiring heavily, you still need replacement fluids. You are also losing water through respiration. You probably know this from your cold weather runs when your face mask, hat, or beard was covered with frost and ice. That was from the water lost from breathing. Dehydration comes easily when skiing — and loss of water can make you more susceptible to frostbite. Hydrate before the tour and drink often. You can carry several water bottles in some of the new packs.

Sip water as you ski

Some skiers carry wineskins on a tour. Be cautious, it is a little like carrying wine in your bike bottle. — surely doesn't help with the balance. Perhaps more serious is the fact that alcohol, as a depressant, can be dangerous in cold conditions. It dilates the blood vessels which lets the skin lose heat faster, leading to potential frostbite problems.

A Safe Return — Days are short in December and January, and it is smart to head back out in plenty of time to clear the trails by dark. The trip will probably be slower on the way back out due to tired legs and arms. You should end with a feeling of, "I could have skied for another hour."

Handling Trouble

While we don't have to deal with nasty dogs, rednecks in pickup trucks, or heat exhaustion in skiing as we might in running, we do face some of the same problems.

Getting Lost — Ever been lost while running in a strange city, in subdivisions where every street or house looked alike? Or gotten into areas during a run where you really feel threatened? In running, if we get a little turned around, we can usually find someone who will give us directions. Not so in the woods.

If you tour in rural country or wilderness areas, you should have someone along who knows how to use a map and compass — and you'd better have the map and compass along with you. There is little chance on many tours of getting lost since you can just follow your tracks back out. But, ski tracks can be wiped out by snowmobiles or new snow or other skiers. There are also times when even if you can find your old tracks, you can still be so turned around as to not be able to tell which way is out.

Winter survival is beyond the scope of this book but there are some fundamentals that runners should know. I call them the four C's — Climb, Confess, Conserve, Communicate. (What works for lost pilots works for lost skiers.)

Climb — If the weather is clear and you have the time and energy, climb a hill and look around. Compare what you see with your map. Look for prominent landmarks — rivers, villages, antennas, McDonald's arches. Don't head out until you are sure of the correct direction.

Know what to do when lost

Confess — Admit that you are lost, or call it "turned around" if you like. Say it out loud to yourself, to your group. Then deal with the problem.

Conserve — Save your energy until you have a plan worked out — don't burn calories by getting panicked. If darkness is near, consider spending the night and start gathering some material for a shelter. (Unless you are experienced, forget about trying to dig a snow cave — they take good snow conditions and are tough to build first try.) Button up your clothing to retain body heat and restrict your movements. Check around for a sheltered spot — an old log with some space under it, a rock outcropping, a cave. Get out of the wind any way you can. If there is no natural shelter to improve, dig a snow trench with your ski tips. Huddle with your friends under an improvised shelter of skis, poles, and boughs and wait for daylight. Running stories like "There I was with a Doberman hanging off my shorts and the owner yelling, "Don't worry, he won't bite!"" can help pass the time.

Communicate — That whistle in your pack can be heard for a good distance so use it. Don't be shy about yelling. Don't waste a lot of energy building massive bonfires or stamping out messages in the snow — that's fine in the movies but you're probably only five miles from your car. Folks will be searching for you so stay put unless you're sure of yourself. If you've let people know where you were going, someone will be looking for you pronto.

Frostbite and Hypothermia

Frostbite is usually caused by wind chill. Runners who hit the roads in winter probably have dealt with frostbite or at least the early stages of it. If your fingers get numb and jaundiced-looking and sting like the blazes when warmed up, that's incipient frostbite. It is even easier to get frostbite while skiing because of the speed involved on the downhills. That's why wind briefs are smart for males and why most ski outfits have panels in the front. Protect exposed skin with creams or a sunblock lotion. If it is frigid, a face mask can be worn. Hats and earmuffs are a must as are mittens or gloves. Mittens are warmer while gloves allow you more freedom with the ski poles.

Watch out for frostbite when touring on wind-swept lakes

I try to warm the extremities before they get too cold. Sometimes, your hands will get really cold during the first 15 minutes of a tour, before you get the body warmed up. I often stop right then, get my hands in close to the body, usually by the armpits (That gets your attention!) and once they are warmed, start out again. Often they will be fine the rest of the day. The point is, deal with it at once.

Stop and warm up hands

Frostbite does not hurt at first. The early warning signs of frostbite, aside from a numb tingly feeling, is a whitish look on the frost-bitten area. Experienced skiers check each other over on cold days. Warm up any frostbitten area, such as the "cold hand on warm skin" technique, and keep checking it. Deep frostbite requires medical attention — don't try to thaw it out, get the skier to immediate medical attention.

Hypothermia is something that most runner/skiers will

never encounter or even necessarily hear of — yet is is worth knowing about because it is potentially so dangerous. It is basically freezing to death — lowering the temperature of the body's core. And it doesn't take sub-zero temperatures. Ever finished a road marathon on a cool day and gotten chilled before you got into dry clothes? That shivering "looking like a ghost" reaction that comes from being exhausted and chilled is the onset of hypothermia. Of course, that is why "space blankets" are handed out after major marathons.

Hypothermia is insidious; it can sneak up on you. Watch for signs of uncontrolled shivering, loss of coordination, or sluggishness among skiers on a tour. If someone has symptoms, get them warmed up, get their body temperature up, and feed them warm food and liquids. Use extra layers of clothing and if there's a sleeping bag around, wrap the person and have one of the group get in as well. Body to body heat has saved many a hypothermia patient.

Dressing in layers, keeping warm and dry, snacking along the way, and skiing within your ability — that's how to prevent hypothermia.

Touring = Fun

Having just run through a litany of calamities, it sounds as if ski touring is like a trip across Antarctica. Touring, as we know, is one of the safest winter activities there is. For runners, there are no vehicles to dodge, no slush to plod through, no overuse injuries to nag, and no high heart rates to tax the system.

Safe and fun

A veteran ski tourer once put it like this, "I am 67 years old and have enjoyed skiing since before it came a popular sport here in Minnesota. I was out there in my beautiful world, mostly by myself, taking photos or bird watching with the binoculars I always had with me. A snack in my backpack extended my stay in places where I wished I could remain forever...."

The camaraderie of friends, the chance to get out with the family for the day, the "tuckered" feeling at the end of the day as you share stories over stew or spaghetti — these are the rewards of touring on skis.

8. Masters racing

A friend and I were standing next to a couple of teenage runners at an informal awards ceremony after a local 10K road race. As age group awards were being handed out, the race director noted the finishing place and time. The young man beside me leaned over to his partner and said, "Boy, these old guys are pretty fast."

The last few years have seen a lot of attention paid to masters running with the addition of speedsters like Bill Rodgers, Frank Shorter, Barry Brown, and Priscilla Welch to the ranks of the 40 and older set. Competition is stiff in most of the masters age groups in road races and so it is with cross country skiing. Except that masters skiing starts ten years sooner, at age 30. Canadian World Cup star Pierre Harvey now races as a masters as do a number of talented U.S. skiers.

Masters are 30 and over

Several years ago, the Inland Empire Ski Club newsletter described a 30K race like this: "One of those Norwegians with an older face on a young body, Einer Svenson, 59 years young, came out from Seattle and smoked everyone. His time was eight minutes ahead of anyone

else." The writer, tongue in cheek, echoed the thoughts of many skiers when she continued, "... I can't wait to get older so I can ski like that."

Older and faster

Masters racing kindles the spark in many older skiers. Dr. John Ayer, now in his early seventies, got "hooked" on cross country citizen racing about 15 years ago, after having been sedentary, except for an occasional game of tennis or downhill ski session, for thirty years prior to that. Ayer has since skied in races all over North America and Europe but he is a realist — he knows that he's not going to be able to ski marathons forever. That's why he packs so much into every day and skis every race that he can squeeze in. "I want to spend the rest of my life convincing people to stop smoking, eat better, and exercise," Dr. Ayer says. "One of the the best ways I can do it by example. If

I learned to skate on skis at age 69, it can convince others that they can."

This competitive enthusiasm has made masters skiing the fastest growing segment of the cross country scene. Many of the younger masters skiers still ski at the U.S. Ski Team level or just below and routinely go up against collegiate skiers. But there is a good mix of masters talent at most citizen races with ability ranging from beginning skier to former Olympic skiers, now in their forties and fifties, who, to the chagrin of their age group rivals, ski like they never stopped training.

Racers of all abilities

Masters age groups are set in five year increments by the U.S. Ski Association and most larger races adhere to the format: 30-34, 35-39, 40-44, 45-49, 50-54, 55-59, 60-64, 65-69, and 70 and older. The older age groups were added because, as USSA's Lee Todd put it, "We've got people moving into their 70's and they didn't want to be competing against one of those 60-year-old 'kids'." As in running, the smaller ski races tend to have 10 year age groups.

Stiff age group racing

There's a good sprinkling of older skiers at many citizen races, people in their 60's and older. Many, as one might imagine, have Scandinavian names and ski as though they grew up on skis, which they probably did. Competition in the younger age groups is fierce, just like in road racing, but the numbers are smaller so you soon learn who is in your age group. And while a new runner/skier might be looked at as "raw meat" by the very competitive ones, you will find that the attitudes are really very supportive.

New skiers are welcomed

Masters racing is a very open group — it's just like the Saturday morning 10K race in many respects. There are some jerks, the same type who sprint to the finish to keep from getting beaten by a female runner, but they are few.

Let's look at the mix in a typical masters race. Up front there are the former ski team folks as well as ski coaches who train every day with their kids. In the middle of the pack are the runners, cyclists, and triathletes who have good motors and are working on their skills. There are some spirited age group battles as skiers, many of whom have dueled each other for decades, in fact sometimes since college, go at it once again. At the back of the pack are the tourers, the skiers who enter a race or two a year, the brand-new skiers, or the out-of-shape skiers. There's room in citizen races for all masters skiers, regardless of ability. Runners will find that they fit right in — and may be surprised at how well they can do the first season.

There are some ski races that, while having masters age groups, are really not citizen races but rather qualifiers for various post-season events. Here you'll find the hot junior skiers, the fast seniors, and perhaps a few ski coaches in the masters groups. If you are over 40 and like me, not too keen about racing against fast 30 year-olds, it might be better to observe rather than getting outclassed. It's not necessarily an ego question, it's more one of staying out of the way of the kids. Most of these races are loops and if you're not careful, you can obstruct a fast-moving young-ster coming up from behind. I like to stand by a coach and

Observe some top racers

listen, you can pick up a lot of good pointers. There are plenty of lower-key races to run — ski those until you get confident on skis.

Aside from open qualifier races and citizen races, there are also a number of races aimed right at masters, or which include masters competition as a major part of the race.

Masters races have keen age group competition

Masters Race Series

Since the late 1970s, masters ski racing has blossomed in the United States through the formation of the Great American Ski Chase, whose races have masters age group awards, and in Canada, through the establishment of the Canadian Ski Odyssey and several regional race series. These masters races are not always special races just for masters, they are often citizen races with masters scoring — sort of a race within a race. Here are some of the major North American series for masters.

There are several regional race series under the auspices of the U.S. Ski Association. The Zak Cup is a series of masters races sponsored by the New England District of the USSA. First known as the Eastern Veterans Cup, it was named for the late Dr. Vlastimil Zak, who epitomized the spirit and camaraderie of masters racing. The Zak series had over a dozen races during its first years but now has settled in at four races, of varying distances, held in the New England states. A skier must belong to USSA to participate in the series.

Zak Cup is oldest race series

A similar race series is held in the Mid-Atlantic states

with seven to eight races scheduled in New York and Pennsylvania. The Mid-West masters program compiles a points list from a host of races across Michigan, Minnesota, and Wisconsin. Most of the other USSA divisions have active masters programs.

Also in the eastern U.S., the New York Ski Racing Association conducts an extensive state-wide series of Empire State Games masters races that culminates in two championship races (one traditional, one freestyle). In Massachusetts, masters championship races, open to state residents, are held at the Bay State Games. The Green Mountain Games in Vermont likewise feature a

Many states have masters programs

championship nordic race. The Laurel Highlands Ski Touring Association, a volunteer organization serving skiers in Pennsylvania, Maryland, and West Virginia, organizes the Allegheny Mountain Race Series of about a dozen races. Many other states have developed similar championships.

The U.S. National Masters Championship, open to any licensed skier, is held each year and consists of both freestyle and traditional races as well as relays over a week-long period. The Canadian Masters Cross-Country Association likewise conducts regional masters competitions and a Canadian National Championship.

World Masters Cup

Until recently, there were few places where masters skiers, unless in good shape and competitive and ready to take on the youngsters, could compete. Veterans classes were sort of an afterthought and there was little age group competition. Some of that changed in the early eighties as a group of Canadians, led by former Olympic decathlon athlete turned skier Bill Gairdner, put together a Canadian masters organization. This began an initiative that

Canadians started it

has spread across the skiing world. Rejecting the term "veteran" as demeaning, Gairdner found strong support for a masters group. He explained, "...we decided that sport retains its highest meaning throughout the span of one's life and that even though aging is universal, the striving for excellence is ageless, and deserves respect regardless of one's physical age. In other words, a champion at any age is still a champion."

In the United States, a sister group was set up by another energetic masters skier, Tom Duffy. Duffy says that members range from college professors to wood-carvers and come from all over the United States. He feels that the most important reason to have a World Masters organization "is the opportunity for masters skiers to meet and compete against each other annually, and to try to achieve each of our personal goals, whether it is to win our age division, or to finish the race in what each feels is our personal best time."

World Masters Cross Country Ski Championships are now held each year and rotate annually between North America, Scandinavia, and Europe. Races are held at 10/ 15K, 20/30 K, 30/50K distances (women ski the shorter lengths) as well as a relay race. When the series is held in North America, the races also serve as the USA-Canada Cup Challenge Series, a competition between U. S. and Canadian masters skiers.

Held annually

It is exciting, yet humbling, to ski against your peers from across the world. The level of competition is keen and many former stars are among the ranks, yet any masters skier can enter and compete. Age groups are started in waves so there is true head-to-head racing. And when the age groups leaders from the older groups, who may have started twenty minutes behind, blow by you like you are standing still, you get a remarkably clear picture of how fast masters skiers can be. World Masters skiing is a fine way to combine a skiing vacation with some challenging racing. These are races that can push you to new PR's.

Wave starts

Masters ski racing, whether at the local level or the World Masters level, has come into its own and represents a great opportunity for runners to compete against ath-letes in their own age group. Masters skiing gives one a chance to rub elbows with an interesting group of runners, cyclists, walkers, canoeists, kayakers, and triathletes who use skiing as a second sport. And along the way, you'll undoubtedly meet some grandfathers and grandmothers who make you think, "I can't wait to get older so that I can ski like that."

Masters skiers are unique

9. Ski 31 miles?

The alarm rings at 3:00 a.m. You pile into the car and are on the road by 3:30, facing a five hour drive, to be there to make a 9:00 a.m. start, ready to ski a 50K marathon. Who else but runners do such nutty things? Why skiers, of course. (And cyclists, canoeists, and triathletes, to name a few.)

Marathon skiing has all the trappings of marathon running — the logistics of getting to the race, long lines at registration, a crowded mass start, and a collective good natured attitude among the participants. People are glad to be there and ready to work hard but have fun doing it. Ski marathons range in size from international happenings with thousands of competitors to small local loppets with only a few hundred racers. The common length is 50 kilometers (31 miles) although many are different lengths, often depending on the trails available at the site. Most marathons also have a half-marathon or shorter option available for those who don't wish to ski the long race.

All sizes and lengths

Aside from length, there are some important differences from road marathons. First, if you are a runner with an

Ski marathons often have a mob scene start

adequate endurance base, you can safely ski a marathon on a limited training schedule. No 65 mile weeks, no 20 mile runs are needed; you can race off what might be considered a 10K training base if you pace yourself. I know, because my first ski marathon was only my second ski race ever, and I finished comfortably in the middle of the pack, tired but not wiped out like I would have been after running a marathon. There's little comparison as to discomfort and potential injury.

No aching legs

The second major difference is that if you don't go out too fast, there's no "wall" to hit. This comes as a surprise to runners since we know what lies in wait for us about 18 to 20 miles into a road marathon, and we tend to expect it while skiing. The last difference is recovery — if you ski smart, you will not have the hobbling, aching legs that characterize most marathon endings as well as the few days afterwards.

Don't be misled, skiing 31 miles as a novice skier is no trip through the park. But it is definitely a reachable goal, even in your first year of skiing. Do not be put off by the distance or your lack of long training ski outings. Thousands of citizen racers complete marathons each year. If you ski wisely, you will not only complete the race, you'll be surprised at how good you feel the following day.

Preparing To Go The Distance

It pays to make the decision to enter a marathon early because there are stiff entry fees that increase as race day nears. It is common to have a $15 to $20 charge several months before the race, and then, as the date approaches, that fee gradually increases to $40 or more. As noted in Chapter 6, you often don't get too much besides a well-run race and a finisher's medal or pin for your money. Don't expect T-shirts or some of the other paraphernalia of road racing. Costs are high when 20-30 miles of trail need to be maintained.

Race day preparation is much like getting ready to run a marathon. Most skiers do some carbo loading the night before — often at the pasta dinner put on by the race organizers. They also glide-wax their skis. (Save grip wax until race day when conditions are better known.) Eat a pre-race breakfast of easily digested food. You'll find that most skiers race on more food then you might consider before a road race. (The energy demands will be higher and it pays to start off well fueled.) Oatmeal, bananas, wheat toast with peanut butter are some of my favorites. When dressing, put some petroleum jelly around the crotch area, the underarms, and the nipples, just as in running, to prevent chafing. It is smart to start hydrating well before the race. I sip on a water bottle in the car on the way to the race and carry it to registration.

Eat a good pre-race meal

Waiting for the bus to the starting line

Arrive at the race site early. Give yourself plenty of time to warm up and check out your skis and wax. Marathon starts are sometimes miles away and there may be a bus ride or some skiing to get to the start, so plan ahead. The wait for the ice cold fiberglass porta-potties can be as bad as a road marathon — and even slower due to the layers that each skier must deal with. As in any ski race, loosen up, do a little stretching, and do a light warmup. Save your energy, it is going to be a long day.

There are several types of starts used in marathons: mass starts just like those used in running where it is everyone for himself or herself, or wave starts where skiers begin in groups, usually age groups, and are timed accordingly. Don't be shy about getting up in the first third of the pack. One runner explained it like this, "After having slower skiers trip and tangle with me for the first couple of kilometers, I vowed never to be so diplomatic about starting again. Now I look for people who look about my speed and make sure I'm up there with them."

Mass start madness

If you love crowds and confusion, you'll have fun at the mass start of a ski marathon. There are many skis clacking against skis, a few falls and entanglements, lots of "sorry" or "easy now" as skiers sort themselves out. Every so often, there is a major pileup, complete with snapped ski poles and frayed tempers. It often takes 5K or so to get things in order but the bottlenecks begin again at the first big hill. The spirit of the racers is great — it is a lot like the first few miles of a big running marathon with everyone pumped up and full of energy. The trick with mass starts is to hang in there, stay upright, and give yourself enough distance on the skier ahead. Relax and conserve energy — one of the things you'll see are racers burning way to much energy trying to pass everyone they can in the first few kilometers. They will pay hours later as the race progresses.

Race Strategy

Pace yourself

One of the strengths that runners bring to marathon skiing is a sense of pace — the ability to listen to the body and race accordingly. "Go out slow and taper off," is the facetious motto of more than one group of runners. For ski marathoning, it is not bad advice. Take the first 5K at a reasonable pace — don't try to do a lot of passing and jockeying for position. The first part of the race, while you are fresh, is a good time to enjoy the day and the racers around you, and consciously work on skiing efficiently.

Unlike road marathons, there is little crowd support except at road crossings and feed stations. There is, however, a lot of mutual support. Skiers chat with one another about the weather, the wax, the course. Chatting is tough with skating because you can not ski side by side on most courses and so it is more a yelling over one's shoulder to converse. On most courses, the trees and terrain provide continual variety and of course, the snow conditions and tracks are always changing. Skiing is a thinking sport and one is always thinking, "What technique works here, how should I best ski this corner?" Just when you have established an effective V-skate, you round a bend and there's a hill to climb. Marathons are a 31 mile mental and physical workout, with work periods and rest periods, challenging and ever-changing.

Drink plenty of liquids during the marathon

When you come to a water stop in a ski marathon, don't be surprised to find warm water or other drink. You may well be offered warm ERG, Gatorade, Kool-Aid, cocoa, or even some warm blueberry concoction. Drink cold water if you can get it or better yet, a good replacement fluid. Most serious skiers have their own "feeds" mixed and available at intervals on the course. Others carry several large bottles with them. Take fluids every 20 minutes or so. I'd

Drink water

drink water early on and save the sugary drinks for late in the race. Most skiers learn to drink on the fly although a short pause during such a long race may be smart.

Replace energy

Aside from not drinking enough fluids, probably the biggest error newcomers make in marathon skiing is not eating (replacing energy). A lot of energy is expended over the four to six hours novices use to complete a long race. During my first marathon, (with half the race to go), it seemed strange to be stuffing brownies in my mouth and washing them down with hot chocolate but it paid off. Eating moderately during races doesn't upset the stomach for most skiers and while new replacement fluids such as EXCEED are favored by some skiers, you will find oranges, corn bread, chocolate chip cookies, and bananas at feeding stations. More than once, in the post-race hubbub you may hear, "I skipped those feeding stations and just plain bonked at the end." This is no time to watch the diet.

As in any long race, there's a certain amount of perseverance needed during the last part of the race. After about 35K or so, it is just a case of concentrating and pushing on. This is where it helps if you have run some marathons. Legs and arms tire and you may go through a "What am I doing this for?" period. There are some things to do to keep going. First, vary your technique. If you are skating, get in the track and double pole for a bit, or marathon skate. Make sure to switch sides while poling, anything to use

Vary your technique

different muscle groups. This is a time for caution. Take the uphills easily, herringbone or diagonal skate them, keeping the heart rate in check.

If you ski a smart race, not only will you finish but, because of the non-pounding nature of skiing, you will feel surprisingly spry afterwards; a bit stiff but nothing like the aftermath of a road marathon. That is why elite skiers can ski a marathon every week during the season and why so many citizen racers ski several 50K races each winter. The "populist" aspect of race series like the Great American Ski Chase and the Canadian Ski Odyssey Series is a tribute to the ease with which a marathon can be skied.

Great American Ski Chase

There are several dozen ski marathons in the United

States each year. The most interesting of these were pulled together in what has to be one of the best things that has happened to long distance citizen racing, the formation of the Great American Ski Chase in 1979. Comprised of the cream of the marathon crop, the Chase truly is a race series for all skiers.

Races are held at locations throughout the country and attract not only hordes of citizen racers but a few dozen elite skiers who "Follow the Chase." For many weekend racers, it is exciting to participate in a race with a skier like Bill Koch or Dan Simoneau. The slick factory-team racing suits, the lithe bodies of top-ranked athletes, and hoopla surrounding Olympic-caliber skiers adds an extra dimension to the race.

Race with the best

The centerpiece of the Great American Ski Chase series is the American Birkebeiner. Patterned after the famous Norwegian Birkebeiner, the race began in 1973 with 74 skiers. It now has more than 7,000 participants. Skiers begin in Hayward, Wisconsin, and after skiing down Main Street, wind through the hills and forests for 55 kilometers to finish in Cable, Wisconsin. Over a quarter of the skiers in the "Birkie" are racing it for the first time. It is a perfect race for a runner to enter for the initial ski marathon.The other GASC races are smaller in size, but each has its unique features.

Canadian Ski Odyssey

There are dozens of Canadian ski marathons, also called loppets, to choose from. They range from the Gatineau 55 in Ottawa, one of the stops on the Worldloppet series, to smaller events strung from Nova Scotia to the Yukon. The emphasis is on participation.

New and popular

Many provinces have a loppet series of their own offering a number of races of varying distances. Such a series is the British Columbia Loppet Series which has a roster of around a dozen races at which racers can earn T-shirts and bronze, silver, and gold pins. Other strong programs have been set up in Quebec, Manitoba, and Alberta.

On a national level, the Cross Country Canada has strung together the premier marathons from across the country into the Canadian Ski Odyssey. The Odyssey

consists of ten events and is aimed at citizen racers. It features passports, in which results are recorded, and awards for completion of the series. Started in 1987, the series attracts 7,000 skiers a year including a number of U.S. skiers.

Worldloppet

If you have ever run a marathon in another country, you will understand the attraction that the Worldloppet has for skiers. Whether you are a top-ranked masters skier or a back-of-the-packer, the chance to compete in a foreign land is an unforgettable experience. And just as runners plan vacations around the London or Paris marathons, so do skiers take winter trips to compete in the original Norwegian "Birkie" or one of the many other international cross country ski races.

The Worldloppet is a series of eleven races held across the world each year. Top ranked long distance skiers in the world compete in these events yet, like the Great American Ski Chase and Canadian Ski Odyssey, the events are aimed at the average citizen racer. And they show up in droves — over 14,000 ski the Finlandia Hiihto and more than 80,000 skiers take part in the series during a typical **Earn a** year. While elite skiers race for the series championship, **medallion** citizen skiers can work toward earning a Worldloppet medallion. To do so, you have to complete the 11 races,

but, you have a lifetime in which to do it. At last count, over 3,000 skiers from countries across the ski world were actively working toward that accomplishment.

The most famous of the Worldloppet races is the Norwegian Birkebeiner, a 55K trek which has been held since 1932. It commemorates the rescue of the child prince Haakon Haakonson by soldiers during a civil war in 1206. The soldiers wore birch leggings and were thus nicknamed "birkebeiners." The race is run on a difficult course between the towns of Lillehammer and Rena in the mountains of central Norway. Skiers wear a 12- pound pack to simulate the weight of the prince. Lillehammer is the site of the 1994 Winter Olympics.

The Birkie

A new international series called the World Classic Grand Prix was begun in 1986 and features eight classical technique races. The races range from 30K to 65K but many have shorter distance options.

Whether you travel across the globe to ski or just sign up for a local loppet, going 31 miles on skis is well within the capability of most runners. The trick is to set a steady pace, take plenty of fluids and food along the way, and enjoy the experience. Don't worry about "racing" the first marathon, that can come later on. Cross country ski marathons are marvelous happenings. You will enjoy the skiers and be pleasantly surprised at how great you feel as you cross the finish line, and how spry you feel the next morning.

10. Waxing basics for runners

Ever been to a big 10K or marathon and been amazed by some of the warmup routines you see? There are often runners performing stretches that defy description, others chanting or aerobic dancing, still one or two others in some yoga position. For beginning road racers, it can be a shock — I remember thinking, "All I know are about two or three stretches. What else can I do?" After a few races, we chalk all this activity to just part of the pre-race hype or nerves — to each, his or her own.

Waxing, whether for ski racing or just a tour, can take on some of the same elements of trendiness. Skiers, like runners, are not above a little "one-upsmanship" and it is easy to make cross country waxing appear to be an advanced course in organic chemistry. It starts like this. First, there's a wax kit that looks well-equipped enough to supply any ski shop, and then you hear something like this: "Well, I found that a soft blue over a special red was just right — I knew the tracks hadn't glazed yet." Or for skating, "I melted three parts yellow to one part graphite and then rilled over the wax." It is enough to drive you

Waxing basics are easy

straight to the no-wax ski sale. But, forget the talk, the mystique. It is easy to learn and master the basics of waxing. Even if you're considering no-wax skis, read on. There are some things that you can do to jazz up the performance of any ski if you know the rudiments of waxing. Here they are.

Getting Ready To Wax

There are two basic categories of wax — glide waxes which are used for skating skis and for the tips and tails of classical skis and grip waxes which are used for the center third of the ski for traditional (diagonal stride) technique. Grip wax is also commonly called kick wax or a kicker. There's a lot going on with glide waxing in performance skiing. All runners who cross country ski should know how to apply glide wax so that will be covered first. But, before we start dripping molten wax on the carpet, let's find a place to do our waxing.

You should have a level surface, preferably waist-high or so, as a platform for waxing. Work benches are fine as are saw horses. Many commercial ski vises are available as well although they are pricey. Find some wooden blocks to set on edge, perpendicular to the work area, to rest the skis

You'll need a wax bench

on. A tailboard that the ski tails can rest against when you scrape the wax is also needed. High performance skis are quite flexible so you will see many types of waxing supports in use before a race. You can use a vise or better yet, two vises, but remember that the ski side walls are fragile. So, with a support for the ski and a work area where you can dribble wax and scrape wax, you are in business.

At the risk of making waxing sound too complicated or expensive, let's look at the basic equipment that a runner should have, or should borrow, to get into waxing. (Don't rush out and buy $50 worth of material, check with your friends.)

> Liquid wax remover — available in ski shops
> Fiberglass or plastic scraper
> Rags — racers use a lint-free material such as
> Fiberlene (SWIX)
> Waxing Iron — an electric iron, preferably
> without steam holes, is best. I have an iron that

I bought for $1.50 at a Salvation Army outlet
(After Ms. Claus said she preferred not to have
ski wax on her silk blouses.)
Fibertex or Scotch Brite Pad
Glide Wax — universal glider or blue/violet
Stiff Plastic Brush
Grip Waxes (see text for recommendations)
Cork

**Electric
irons
work best**

Waxing material can add up in price, so buy only what
you need and borrow the rest.

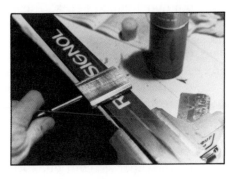

This type of waxing iron is
heated with a torch

Glide Waxing

Regardless of your type of skiing or your type of skis, you
will want to learn how to prepare the gliding surface of your
skis. This will be the tips and tails for all skis and the whole
ski bottom for skating skis. Glide wax will not only jazz up
the performance of your skis, it will also help protect the
bottoms.

**Wax the
glide
surfaces**

In the days of wooden skis, pine tar was used to seal the
pores of the base. This smelly, smoky process, utilizing
torches, gunky rags, and gooey pine tar, was a satisfying
part of the ski preparation ritual for many skiers. The smell
of pine tar evokes special memories for many old-time and
not so old-time skiers. Since the advent of fiberglass skis,
glide wax has taken over for pine tar and while the smell
is not so pungent, the skis are much faster.

Glide waxing took a page out of the alpine skiers'
handbooks when nordic racers began, over a decade ago,
to iron glide wax onto their new plastic skis. But alpine wax

is designed for short fast dashes down the slope and couldn't hold up for the longer cross country races, so a whole new generation of nordic glide waxes was developed. At first, there were only a few gliders, but now there is a rainbow of wax colors and special additives that can mystify the newcomer. Glide waxing technique can take on some of the "mystique" that was once reserved for grip waxing. But don't get too fancy. A wide-range (both in temperature and snow conditions) glider, such as purple, will fit the bill for most skiing.

Try purple glider

Modern cross country skis have bases made of polyethylene or similar material, commonly called P-Tex. These bases, regardless of the material, look smooth to the eye but actually have countless microscopic pores. Before we glide wax, we want to clean the base to remove any dirt or old wax. Then we will proceed to fill those tiny pores with glide wax.

If the ski has previously been waxed, remove as much wax as you can with a plastic scraper. Draw it from tip to tail, curling the wax off. Then clean the base with a wax remover solvent and a rag or Fiberlene. Let the solvent soak in and then remove it with the wiper. Be cautious with solvents — they are volatile so keep them off your skin and work in a ventilated space. Once the skis are dry, you can get ready to apply glide wax. Some experts recommend using a molten glide wax to clean the ski instead of a solvent. To do this, you iron a warm glide wax, such as orange, onto the surface and before it cools, scrape it off.

Clean the skis first

Another development in nordic skiing that has evolved with ski skating is the concept of structure for the ski base. Skis that appear as smooth as glass are never as fast as skis that have some texture, some grooves. Visualize a couple of panes of glass placed together with a film of water between them. Suction makes them very difficult to pull apart. The same goes for skis, which ride on a thin film of water. Look at a racer's ski and you will see a series of tiny grooves, not unlike phonograph grooves, down the length of the ski. The warmer and wetter the snow, the more the need for structure to break up the thin layer of water between the snow and the ski.

Rilling is the term used for pressing thin grooves into

skis. This is done by racers with a special tool, a riller. Fine grooves are put in for cold conditions while wider ones are used when conditions are warmer. For our purposes, a medium sandpaper (carbide paper if available) wrapped around a cork and drawn from tip to tail along the glide portions of the ski, will be more than adequate. Then lightly buff the tips and tails, or the whole ski for skating, with a Fibertex or Scotch Brite pad. This is a little like scrubbing with a face cloth. It removes the tiny hairs from the sanding and also helps open up the pores. So, with a clean ski which now has some tiny longitudinal grooves in the base, we are ready to wax. For most runner/skiers, a structuring and glide waxing treatment will last for weeks, if not for months. This is definitely a "set it and forget it" task.

Add some structure

As noted before, glide wax is applied to the tips and tails on no-wax skis. The center area, which will be either the no-wax pattern or the grip zone, is left untouched. For no-wax skis, you also have the option of using a liquid solution such as MAXIGLIDE® which can be wiped on.

For classical skis, you must locate the "grip zone," for that will be left unwaxed and ready for kick waxing. This area runs from about eighteen inches in front of the binding to the heel plate. Your ski shop can help you determine this — remember the "paper test"? If you can find a truly flat surface, stand on the skis and have someone mark where the paper stops sliding. That determines the position of the zone. Mark it on each ski sidewall before you glide wax.

Glide waxes are color-coded to match snow conditions, but are much less sensitive to temperature and snow conditions than grip waxes. Find yourself a bar of violet or blue glide wax — it will be fine for recreational skiing. Glider is melted on with an iron. An electric iron with an adjustable temperature is the best bet. Waxing irons that are heated with a torch are fine for pre-race waxing in a parking lot but are hard to keep at a regulated temperature. Whatever you use, watch the heat — ski bases can be ruined by too much heat. I have had the base surface lift on two different skis over the years — it's a good way to develop an ulcer. Use a temperature that will melt the wax

Melting glide wax on with an electric iron

but not make it smoke. Err on the side of coolness — it will only take you a little longer to finish the task. Never, in spite of what you may see experienced skiers do, run a torch directly on the ski base. Elite racers have had years of experience and also have the luxury of a bag of racing skis provided by their sponsor.

Drip dots of glide wax on both sides of the groove in the glide zones, which will be the whole ski for skaters, and then run the iron back and forth, working a section of the ski at a time. The object is to spread the wax in a molten layer and let it penetrate the pores of the ski. That means keeping the iron moving and the wax liquid for a while — some coaches recommend two or three minutes. Watch the heat, pulling the iron away if the underside (top) of the ski starts getting too warm. Check under the extreme tip or tail, the very thin section — it should be warm but not

Keep the iron moving

hot. Add wax as it is absorbed. When the skis have been waxed, set them aside to cool for a half hour or so. Then you will get to remove most of the wax that you have just melted on. (Note: Some skiers "crayon" on their wax rather than drip it on — to save wax. Some also wipe/scrape the wax off while it is still warm. Some hard gliders, START Green or REX Blue for example, require this but most should be scraped after cooling.)

Once the bases have been cooled, scrape all but a very thin layer of the glide wax off the bases. Do this with a sharp plexiglass scraper (which can be sharpened by drawing it along a file) using a steady pressure from tip toward the tail. Keep the pressure light and make multiple drawings of the scraper down the ski. This is a good thing to watch when hanging out at ski areas or ski races. You will note that nearly all the ski prep actions — cleaning, waxing, scraping, rilling — are done down the ski. The theory is that you'll get the molecules lined up the right way, which sounds good enough to me to do. Draw the scraper down the ski base until most of the wax is gone. Don't worry about taking too much off — you want to be skiing on the wax in the pores. Don't forget to remove the hardened wax from the groove and the sidewalls as well.

Scrape from tip to tail

Brushing is the final step in glide waxing

To finish up the ski preparation, runners who want fast skis can take a nylon brush and brush the base, again from tip to tail. This removes the wax from the rills, opening them up. You should see a light dusting of wax as you brush. Now run the Fibertex or Scotch Brite pad lightly down the ski and you are ready to go. This application of glide wax should be good for days of skiing. If the tracks are icy and harsh, the wax will wear faster. You will note a faint whiteness or white streaks on the bases and then it will be time to get out the iron again.

Personalize your skis

Runners may forego the work of glide waxing, figuring that their skis are fast enough already. But glide waxing is easy to learn and usually has to be done only a few times a season for non-racers. It gives you a chance to check over your skis, to "personalize" them for your use. This tinkering with ski bottoms is, for many skiers, an integral part of preparation for skiing, ranking just behind training. It is something that some runners will take the time to do while others ignore. But the first time that you are passed on a shallow downhill by someone with comparable gear, you'll think twice about ignoring glide wax. We work too hard going up the hills not to get the most out of going down them. And, fast skis also go uphill faster than slow skis.

Grip Waxing

Wax is color-coded

Grip wax, the wax under your ski boot, provides the "get up and go" for the diagonal stride and other classical techniques. Waxes come in small tins and are color-keyed to the snow condition and temperature. When your skis are waxed properly, each kick and glide moves you effortlessly down the track and all is right with the world. But on the other hand, if your wax is too hard for the snow, you'll slip and slide, and curse the day you ever tried waxing. At the other extreme, if your skis have the glide of a trowel over wet concrete and every pine needle and twig on the trail is now on the bottom of your skis, you've probably got wax that is way too soft for the snow. These are the horror stories from the dark side of grip waxing. But if you understand the basics, you can learn to wax for every condition and correct problems if they occur. But to do that, you have to understand a little about how kick wax actually works.

Wax basics

The type of snow determines which kick wax should be used. Remember the pictures by "Snowflake" Bentley, how each snow crystal had an array of spiky points? With new snow, these sharp spikes penetrate ski wax easily, and we can use a hard wax (like a green or a blue) for crisp fresh snow conditions. With warmer snow, a warmer wax such as a purple might be in order. Snow that is good for snowballs also has rounded surfaces and thus calls for a soft wax like a red. And when the snow has melted and refrozen, the crusty icy surfaces call for klister wax, the sticky wax that comes in tubes like toothpaste. To make things interesting, there are 29 different waxes, each at $3.50 a tin, available from one major brand (SWIX). While this can make waxing appear to be an alchemist's fantasy, the basics come down to this: the kick wax needs to be soft enough to let the snow crystals penetrate when you put your full weight on the ski for the pushoff, yet it must be hard enough to allow the ski to glide cleanly.

Warm snow, warm wax

Waxing will vary in different parts of the country. Some

A hard grip wax is used in cold conditions

areas in the West, blessed with uniform powder conditions day after day, are a breeze for waxing. Skiers rub a little Extra Blue and hit the trails for another outing. ("Extra" waxes are a little softer, e.g., Extra Blue is softer than Blue. Conversely, "Special" waxes have a little colder range.) Cross country trekkers in the Pacific Northwest get to know their warm red waxes quite well while skiers in the

Northeast deal with klister for much of the late winter. Talk to your skier friends and see what they use, what tins of wax are nearly gone. This will give you a good idea of what to start with. Here are some suggestions:

Basic wax options

Option 1   "Two Wax" System — One for dry snow, one for wet
             Universal Klister — for refrozen snow

Option 2   Special Green, Extra Blue, Violet, Special Red, Extra Red
             Universal Klister, Purple Klister

Each wax has a temperature range, usually in Celsius, listed on the tin, and each wax manufacturer has small charts which should be available when you buy wax. Most skiers use a small thermometer to determine snow and air temperature.

Skis are easiest to wax when dry and warm. The key with grip waxing is to crayon on a light layer of wax and then use the cork to rub it in until you can hardly see it. Add a couple more thin layers, corking each one. Then, try them for a bit. If the wax slips a little, perhaps just a thicker layer will give you the grip you want. You can also run the wax a little longer on the ski. Or you may want to rub on a layer of the next warmer wax you have. If your skis stick, you need a harder wax. Put a layer on over the warmer and cork it in.

There are a couple of other things to keep in mind:

1. Let your skis cool before you check the wax. It takes a while for the wax to set, and if you try them right after waxing, you might get a false reading.

2. If you are skiing in humid conditions, you'll find that you need a softer wax than you might expect from the temperature reading. (Extra Blue, with its wide range, works in many higher humidity ski days.)

3. Breaking trail and touring in back country allows you to wax a little colder than for the prepared tracks.

Klister. Most skiers have wrestled with klister-laden skis and ended up with the gooey mess on parkas, ski bags, car seats, you name it. Klister has a bad reputation and deserves it. Yet, when the snow melts and the crystals loose their points, and then it refreezes, klister is the only

Spring skiing may require klister wax

wax that is effective. Soft klisters like red and violet are easy to apply if the tube is warm. Dab it on lightly in dots and use the applicator to spread it on a thin film. Universal klister, with its wide range, is a good bet for warm temperatures while purple is more suited for the colder ones. Remove klister after each ski session with wax remover before you put the skis in the car.

Klister is for refrozen snow

So for runners who choose to wax, it's easy to get some better performance out of classical or skating skis with some good base structure and some glide wax. Kick waxing, once the basics are understood, is certainly not quantum physics. It has a certain "bubble, bubble, toil, and trouble" reputation that is undeserved. You can make it very complicated — or you can make it uncomplicated by understanding how to use a few basic waxes. A runner's motto for waxing should be "KISS": Keep It Simple, Skier.

# 11. On the road again

Cross country skiing comes to a peak in late February/ early March in the Eastern U.S. and in late March in the West and throughout Canada. As the sun gets higher in the sky, runners start itching to shed winter windsuits and go out and run bare-legged. Runners who have skied all winter feel ready to go out and "burn up the track." But they're not as ready as they think.

Writer Hal Higdon, known for his masters running, is also an accomplished cross country skier. When asked if there are benefits for runners from skiing cross country, he responded, "Yes, if it allows you to rest injured running muscles. No, if you come back too soon in the spring and injure yourself again."

Higdon's point is that for some runners, the risks in cross country skiing are not found on icy trails or tree-lined curves, they lie on the sun-dried roads of early spring. As the snowbanks recede there is a tendency to run too much. Coach Daly explains, "Runners tend to go overboard in early spring and try to run every day."

A lot depends on how often you have been able to run

Spring tours are warm and enjoyable

during the winter. If you've run several times a week, the switch to running is easier. Still you have to fight the tendency to overtrain. The transition back to running in the spring is a time for moderation. Even though you may feel like an aerobic horse after a winter's worth of skiing, your legs need time to adjust to the pounding. This is not the time to get hurt.

Terry Aldrich, the highly successful coach of running and skiing at Middlebury College, recommends caution in the spring. "The transition from skiing to running has to be a very, very, very careful one," Aldrich says. "If skiers haven't been running during the winter, even though their cardiovascular systems are fully developed, their running muscles just aren't there. You can do some real damage as far as overuse injuries. If you jump into it too quickly and try a 60 mile week, you'll be bedridden."

Be careful getting started

Potential problem areas are shin splints, Achilles soreness, tendinitis, or soreness in the hip area. Your legs will feel sore after workouts and will have little springiness. This is a time for patience. It is also a good time to make sure that your training flats are well-cushioned and that you are extra careful with warmups and stretching.

Coach Aldrich, himself a 2:40 marathoner and 33:00 10K runner, recommends a very gradual progression. "I try to start easy — I've learned that through experience.

Unless you have been running, start with a mile or two, every other day. Increase it slowly each week until you get your legs under you. It takes about a month."

One way to help with the transition is to stay on your skis. Spring is a great time to keep skiing as you pick up the running mileage on the other days. Skating comes into its own on the firm corn snow of spring. Touring is more fun — the sun is higher and the days are longer. Not only is it more comfortable weather-wise, there are fewer skiers. Just when the first flowers are blooming in the suburbs, some of the best skiing is found back in the woods.

Add mileage slowly

Run every other day or two days on and one off. Keep the intensity low through the first month as you build leg strength. On the off days from running, I like to ski or get out on my mountain bike.

Every runner transitions differently. Some can build up the mileage fast and stay injury free. I know that I have to be very cautious and patient with my spring running. My masters legs let me know when I'm overdoing it — and I limp and ache — something I haven't done for a whole ski season. But being careful pays off. With the aerobic base from skiing and a spring tuneup of the running muscles, you can really be ready by the time running season hits full swing. And very likely, when the dog days of summer are upon you, you will be thinking about beginning to train for your second season — the season of cross country skiing.

Glossary

Aerobic   Skiing "with oxygen" at a pace within the training heart rate.

Anaerobic   "Without oxygen." Also called oxygen debt.

Bail   The metal piece on a three-pin binding that clamps the boot to hold it to the ski.

Base Prep   The flattening, structuring, and waxing of a ski base to make it fast.

Basket   The device attached to the bottom of the ski pole to keep the pole from sinking into the snow.

Biathlon   A rapidly growing sport with combines marksmanship and cross country running or skiing. (Not to be confused with the run/bike/run event of the same name.)

Bill Koch Ski League   The youth program of the U.S. Ski Association.

Binder Wax   Also called base wax, used to make grip wax wear longer.

Bounding   Running, usually uphill, using bounding motions to simulate diagonal stride or skating.

Camber   The arch built into skis to support the skier's weight while allowing the ski to glide.

Carbon fiber   A material used in ski pole shafts and skis.

CCC   Cross Country Canada, the nordic arm of the Canadian Ski Association.

Chair dip   A dip down between two chairs. Used to strengthen the arm muscles and shoulders.

Christie   A skidding turn on both uphill ski edges.

Citizens race   A ski race for everyone. Called a loppet in Canada.

Classical   See *Traditional*

Compression   The upper body movement that powers ski poling.

Cork   A block of cork (often synthetic) that is used to polish grip wax.

Diagonal stride   The classic cross country technique, similar to walking or running, where the arm and opposite leg swing forward together.

Double camber   The center section of classical skis where the camber is stiffer.

Double poling   Propelling oneself forward with both poles. An important technique for all skiers, not just racers.

F.I.S.   Federation International de Ski, the international governing body for skiing.

Fall line   The shortest line up or down the hill.

Fannypack   A small pack with a belt, also called a bumbag.

Fartlek "Speed play." Changing speeds during a workout, whether running or skiing.

Feed   A drink for athletes such as defizzed cola, ERG, or MAX.

Flat ski   Skiing with the surface flat on the snow. Essential in skating.

Flex   How easily a ski bends.

Free Skating   Skating without poling. Used on flats and some descents.

Gaiters   Waterproof cuffs used to keep snow out of ski boots.

Glide wax   A hard wax used on the tips and tails of classical skis and on the whole base for skating.

Glycogen   The substance stored in muscles and used up in long races.

Grip   The thrust onto the snow that propels a skier forward in the diagonal stride. Also called *kick.*

Gunde Skate   Also called V-2 alternate or open field skate, the skier glides before poling on one side.

Hard wax   Solid grip wax, such as Special Green, used for cold snow.

Heart monitor   A training device strapped across the chest which determines heart rate. Usually has a wrist watch display.

Heel Plate   A plate or disk with ridges to keep ski boot heel in place when weight is on the ski.

Herringbone   A "V-walking" movement used to climb steep hills.

Hypothermia   A decrease in body temperature caused by exposure.   A potentially serious problem for skiers or runners.

Imagery   A "psyching" technique used to get ready to compete.

Jackrabbit Ski League   Canada's successful youth ski program.

Kick   See Grip.

Kick turn   A method of reversing direction when standing still on skis.

Kinesthetic sense   Awareness of what is happening to the body.

Klister   A sticky liquid wax used for ice and refrozen snow conditions.

Knickers   Knee length ski pants, used with long socks.

Lactic acid   The substance generated at a rate faster than the body can assimilate when runners/skiers go anaerobic.

Layering   Dressing for skiing in layers, usually three. (Wicking, insulation, protection.)

Loppet   A "people's race." Called a *citizens race* in the U.S.

Marathon skate   A skating motion used with prepared tracks.

Masters   Runners over 40, skiers over 30.

MaxVO2   A measure of the capacity of the oxygen system.

Mohair   A hairy material used in strips to provide grip.

Negative Base   A patterned waxless base cut into the ski.

Nordic combined   An event combining ski jumping and XC racing.

No-wax skis   Skis that get their grip from a patterned bottom, chemical base, or some other non-wax system.

Offset   A Canadian term for a V-skating technique used on hills. Called V-1 in U.S.

One-skate   A skating method for the flats, also called V-2. Requires lots of energy and good balance.

Orienteering   Navigation with map and compass to preselected points. Both running and skiing events are gaining popularity in North America.

Overboots   Light covers that pull over ski boots. Used over racing boots in cold or wet conditions.

Oxygen debt   Going past the anaerobic threshold in exertion.

P-tex   A polyethylene base material used for ski bases.

P-tex candle   A stick of plastic which can be melted to repair scratches or gouges on ski bases.

Paper test   A method of evaluating camber/stiffness of skis in relation to a skier's weight and ability.

Pine tar   A black gooey substance that is used to prepare the base on wooden skis.

Plyometrics   Lengthening a muscle (stretching it) before it contracts.

Positive base   A patterned ski base where the grip surface protrudes from the base.

Pulk   A sled pulled by a skier to move kids or provisions.

Pulley   A simple way to strengthen arms for poling.

Rilling   Pressing or cutting fine ridges into the base of the ski to reduce the suction of wet snow.

Roller skis   Short skis with rubber-tired wheels used in off-season.

Rollerboard   A "do-it-yourself" device for building upper body strength.

Sidecut   The reduction in ski width in the midsection that aids turning.

Sideslip   Sliding downhill sideways with control.

Siitonen technique   Another name for marathon skating, after Pauli Siitonen, an early ski skater.

Skate turn   A turn where the skier skates off a weighted ski.

Skateblades   Plastic molded hockey skates with three to five small in-line wheels popular for ski skating practice.

Ski striding   Running or walking with ski poles.

Skins   Long mohair strips that are stuck or strapped to skis to climb. Used primarily in mountaineering skiing.

Slideboard   A training system used by speed skaters as well as some skiers. Often a formica countertop with padded sidewalls.

Specificity   Training aimed at developing skills and muscles for a particular sport.

Step turn   A turn where the ski tips are picked up and moved, one at a time, in a new direction.

Strong side   The side on which you are poling when skating V-1.

Telemark   A skiing method featuring turns with flexed knees and the outside ski ahead of the inside ski.

Training effect   The exercise level needed to derive benefits, usually 60 to 70% of maximum heart rate.

Traditional   One of the names for the diagonal stride and other "in-track" techniques. Also called *classical.*

Transition snow   Snow at the freeze/thaw zone.

Traverse   To ski across the hill at an angle to the fall line.

Triathlon   A winter event combining running, skiing, and biking.

Tuck   A crouching downhill position used to cut wind resistance.

Two-wax system   A simplified grip wax system with one wax for dry snow and one for wet snow.

USSA   U. S. Ski Association.

V-skate   The skating herringbone that fis the basis of skating methods.

Wax pocket   The center section of the ski base for grip wax.

Wind chill   Equivalent temperature when wind velocity is considered.

Where to get more information

Books

Brady, Michael. *Cross-Country Ski Gear*   2nd ed.
    The Mountaineers, 1987

Brady, Michael. *Waxing And Care Of Cross-Country Skis*
    Wilderness Press, 1984

Borowski, Lee. *Ski Faster, Easier*
    Leisure Press, 1986

Caldwell, John. *The New Cross-Country Ski Book* 8th ed
    The Stephen Greene Press, 1988

Caldwell, John and Brady, Michael. *Citizen Racing*
    The Mountaineers, 1982

Cross Country Canada. *The National Guide To Loppet Skiing*
    Cross Country Canada, 1985

Gillette, Ned and Dostal, John. *Cross Country Skiing* 3rd ed.
The Mountaineers, 1988

Hall, Marty. *One Stride Ahead*
Winchester Press, 1981

Hall, William. *Cross Country Skiing Right*
Harper & Row, 1985

Mansfield, Dick. *Skating On Skis*
Acorn Publishing, 1988

Woodward, Bob. *Cross-Country Ski Conditioning*
Contemporary Books, 1981

Sharkey, Brian J. *Training For Cross Country Ski Racing*
Human Kinetics, 1984

Videos

How To Ski
Good basic technique info from the makers of Karhu skis.

Nordic Ski School
A four part series with clear descriptions and good demonstrations issued by the National Collegiate Ski Association.

Simple Secrets Of Skating
A "home-grown" look at skating from the 1989 USSA Ski Coach Of The Year, Lee Borowski.

Skating Away With Bill Koch
Beautiful scenery and exciting technique shots with America's Olympic medalist.

Skating With Gunde
Instruction and tips from one of the world's best skiers.

World Cup '88
Great racing shots of skating and traditional techniques along with dryland training advice.

Periodicals

Cross Country Skier
A five times a year look at ski technique and equipment from the people who bring you *Runner's World.*

The Master Skier
A tabloid presentation of topics for skiers over 30.

Nordic West
Articles for skiers in western U.S.. and Canada.

Mail Order Firms

Eagle River Nordic
Box 936, Eagle River, WI 54521
1-800-423-9730

L. L. Bean
Freeport, Me 04033
1-800-221-4221

Nordic Equipment, Inc.
Box 997, Park City, Utah 84060
1-800-321-1671

Reliable Racing Supply, Inc.
624 Glen Street, Glens Falls, NY 12801
1-800-223-4448

National Ski Organizations

United States Ski Association
Box 100
Park City, Utah 84060
801-649-9090

Cross Country Canada
1600 James Naismith Drive
Suite 40
Gloucester, Ontario K1B 5N4
613-748-5662

Index